During his days in the field, Damian Marrett lectured in various undercover policing courses around Australia. Since leaving the force he has worked as a consultant for the Nine Network television drama *Stingers*.

UNDERCOVER

UNDERCOVER
DAMIAN MARRETT

HarperCollins*Publishers*

HarperCollins*Publishers*

First published in Australia in 2005
by HarperCollins*Publishers* Australia Pty Limited
ABN 36 009 913 517
A member of the HarperCollins*Publishers* (Australia) Pty Limited Group
www.harpercollins.com.au

Copyright © Damian Marrett and Michael Blayney 2005

The right of Damian Marrett and Michael Blayney to be identified as the moral rights authors of this work has been asserted by them in accordance with the *Copyright Amendment (Moral Rights) Act 2000* (Cth).

This book is copyright.
Apart from any fair dealing for the purposes of private study, research, criticism or review, as permitted under the Copyright Act, no part may be reproduced by any process without written permission.
Inquiries should be addressed to the publishers.

HarperCollins*Publishers*
25 Ryde Road, Pymble, Sydney, NSW 2073, Australia
31 View Road, Glenfield, Auckland 10, New Zealand
77–85 Fulham Palace Road, London W6 8JB, United Kingdom
2 Bloor Street East, 20th Floor, Toronto, Ontario M4W 1A8, Canada
10 East 53rd Street, New York, NY 10022, USA

National Library of Australia Cataloguing-in-Publication data:

Marrett, Damian.
  Undercover.
  ISBN 0 7322 8108 3.
  1. Marrett, Damian. 2. Undercover operations – Australia.
  3. Police – Australia – Biography. 4. Criminal investigation –
  Australia. I. Title.
363.2320994

Cover design by Darren Holt, HarperCollins Design Studio
Cover photographs from the collection of Damian Marrett
Internal design by Darian Causby
Typeset in 12 on 14.5pt Bembo by Kirby Jones
Printed and bound in Australia by Griffin Press

70gsm Classic used by HarperCollins*Publishers* is a natural, recyclable product made from wood grown in sustainable forests. The manufacturing processes conform to the environmental regulations in the country of origin, Finland.

10 9 8 7   09 10

Acknowledgments

Well, here goes nothing. I guess it's a good time to clear out the clutter in the filing cabinet upstairs. Bundle up the old stuff; make some room for the new. That's the plan anyway.

To the best of my knowledge everything that follows is factual. A few names and places may have been altered for legal or personal reasons, but I'm committed to giving an insider's account of my life undercover.

I always took a lot of pride in my undercover work, but there was no bravery in anything I did. When I first took on the job my contribution felt like it was equal parts ego, bravado and naivety — not three of the greatest motivating forces. By the end of my tenure, the work became an addiction, always looking for bigger and bigger busts.

I wasn't the undercover operative's undercover operative by any stretch, if you know what I mean. Often I would become easily bored, on occasions taking stupid risks. I also cranked up the danger factor for cheap thrills sometimes. Not the brightest idea when you're dealing with blokes who'd sooner kill you than deal with crap.

During those years, I also saw the blackest of black in people. Greed and hatred can consume just about anyone. There was a real down side associated with the job; paranoia, guilt, conflict, anger, loneliness and a sense of loss all sat just below the surface.

But I also had some of the best times of my life. I have the utmost respect for the working copper's dedication and efforts. Too often these attributes go largely unrewarded, even unnoticed. Police officers are frequently criticised by those with much less understanding of the job's perils and pitfalls. To those people with bleeding hearts and mush for brains, well, you can go and get stuffed for all I care.

And as for the crooks who felt betrayed by what I did to them, just a reminder that your job was to take risks, and you were paid handsomely for your troubles. My only job was to catch you. Everyone knows that undercovers are out there working on crooks, so don't blame me for your failings. You're the ones getting paid the big bucks. It'd be an easy job if there were no chances of getting caught.

Having said that, in a strange way I could identify with some crooks. Imagine always living on your toes, taking huge risks, never being able to fully trust anyone, not knowing who'll be coming through your door next, coppers or criminals. At the very least, most of them knew the rules of the game — if you do the crime, you've got to be prepared to do the time.

And to those who think that dealing drugs is a glamorous lifestyle, just cast your eye over the current death toll in Melbourne's underworld war.

Anyway, thanks to the tireless Michael Blayney. His patience will be rewarded in the afterlife. Maybe.

And thank you to the following for your encouragement and support over the years: Murph, Michelle, Coach, Googa, Strawny, Kim, Jack, Vic, Jackie, Georgia, Kirsty, Laura, Chris, Paul, Tony, Peta, Nick, Brit, Ragnhild, Thor, Marit, Tania, Lil, Henry, Hong Kong Mike, Tiger Tank Gav, Benno, the Napier Street boys, the Abbotsford tearaway, and to my mother and family far and wide.

*In loving memory of my father, Brian Francis.
A life unfairly cut short.*

One

1985-1991

For six years, my life was one big lie. Actually it wasn't just the one lie; there were hundreds and hundreds of them. I told them for a living. They tumbled effortlessly out of my mouth, and when I was at the top of my game, no one, least of all me, gave them a second consideration as they manipulated their intended targets.

Of course, over those six years I had a form slump or two. There were times when I questioned the nature of the work, and my role in it. For instance: what other field rewards bullshit artists? Used car sales, politics and law, just off the top of my head. I was all too aware that I wasn't travelling in the best company.

Paraphrased, the job description of a Victoria Police undercover operative reads rather simply: ingratiate, establish trust, dump person in shit. Sometimes, especially on lengthy jobs, I'd find myself ingratiating a bit too much, and I'd end up feeling guilty when the shit-dumping was on the agenda. The psychologists used to call this sort of behaviour 'Stockholm syndrome'. I just thought it was second nature.

Yet despite all the guilt (and the lies), I managed to play a role in over fifty operations, often working up to three or four jobs at the one time. Some operations were intricate and involved, played out on a grand scale. Others were so small that, when I read through my old police diary, I have trouble recalling any of the details.

But there's one thing I do know about every last one of those jobs: I was just being me.

Some people think you need a degree from NIDA to work as an undercover cop. But from my experience, acting is just that — acting. I found that undercover work was just a matter of tapping into different facets of my personality when required. For the most part, good undercovers will pretty much be themselves, revealing only what's necessary to get the job done. That's not denying that your primary aim is to manipulate a target, but everyone has a capacity to manipulate. Kids do it every day. If you wanted a bike for your birthday, you had to take your parents along for the ride as well.

Undercover work was never something I actively pursued. One minute I was a young cop in uniform, the next I was an undercover Drug Squad detective. It all happened so rapidly that I barely had time to comprehend what I was doing, or any of the consequences. Looking back, I'm just happy that I managed to bullshit my way through criminal circles without making a complete fool of myself.

And even though my expectations weren't particularly lofty, I'm proud of one thing: I was always eager to learn. Right from the outset, I wanted to be the best undercover operative I could possibly be.

A good undercover has to process information in the most pressured of circumstances and environments. On top of that, you have to be able to act on three or four things at the same time. A drug dealer might say he wants to sell me some smack outside a video store on Smith Street, Collingwood. I'd be taking this in, but my mind would be racing: 'Why does he want to do it there? If I were a crook, would I want to do it there? Will it lock me in to doing further deals at that same location? Is the area surveillance-friendly? Will the surveillance cameras capture my best side?'

Once a relationship with a target was established, part of my job was to pick up on things that he would want from me — qualities he admired or expected from a fellow crook. When those signals presented themselves, I'd just give him what he wanted.

Maybe a target had hired me as a hitman. Some personality traits are expected when you pose as a gun for hire. Well, I found there wasn't any great demand for warm and cuddly hitmen. So I'd sometimes put on a show, if that meant keeping the operation's objectives on the right track. It could be as simple as a no-nonsense stare after the target (the bloke we were hoping to arrest at the end of the whole job) said something I didn't like.

Although one time I posed as a hired killer with a thing for flowers. It just seemed right at the time, and I didn't mind screwing with the stereotype.

'You can't be doing this job forever,' the target said to me one day.

'I'll be right. I've been saving up.'

'What are you gonna do then?'

'Open a florist's shop.'

'Flowers?' he said, laughing at the thought of a hitman gift-wrapping daffodils for little old ladies.

'I like flowers,' I said, fixing him with a set of cold eyes that looked like they were already reaching for a gun. 'What's wrong with liking flowers?'

In other situations the targets might have preferred to do business with a clever bloke. I tried my best on that score. I remember once doing the sums on a piece of paper for a brain-dead smack dealer: 'How to Deal Drugs 101' by Damian Marrett.

Or sometimes I had to act a bit vague to get people to open up. By that I mean I'd play dumb if I was trying to glean information. And besides, when I played dumb, I sometimes got more on a listening device anyway. 'Okay, can you run that deal by me again? From the beginning. Louder.'

Like most people, I often wonder what sort of person I would be now if my life had taken a different direction. At seventeen, I was convinced that I would be a bookmaker. My father was an accountant, and I had toyed with that idea as well, but the lure of the betting ring excited me far more than crunching numbers in an office. I'd also considered joining the police force but, to be honest, I hadn't given it too much serious thought.

In 1985 I had a part-time job running around country tracks, laying off bets for my bookie boss. It was good fun. I was happy, and it seemed like the bookie's life was for me. One drunken night, however, fate intervened on my behalf.

After well and truly tying one on at a party, I stupidly jumped in my old Ford XY station wagon. Hard to justify now, but drink-driving was almost a rite of passage back in the eighties.

Hurtling along Banyule Road in Melbourne's northeast, I lost control on the first bend I negotiated, rolling the car in the process. It finally finished up on its roof, a total write-off. Somehow I got out of the wreck in one piece, and stumbled back up the road to the party. A quick drink to calm the nerves and I was tucked safely into bed.

The next morning I woke up with a hangover that refused to go away. A friend drove me to the car. It wasn't there. By the time I made it home the police had already put in an appearance, checking in with my mum and dad.

Undercover

They'd found the car; now they were looking for me. So, after copping an earful from the parents, I was off to Heidelberg police station for another grilling.

When I got there, this old-school copper went to town on me. *You will be charged, you will lose your licence.* I was quietly taking this all in when I caught sight of a poster on the wall. A recruitment poster. It was a long shot, but I figured it was worth a shot.

'Will this affect my chances of joining up?' I asked as innocently as I could without coming across as a suck.

'What?' I don't think he expected my query.

'Will I still get accepted for the academy?'

'Don't tell me you want to join up,' he said incredulously.

I dropped the bottom lip in a half-quiver and put on a long, sad face. The one that's got *bullshit* written all over it in invisible ink. 'Well yeah, it's been kind of a dream of mine for years.'

He studied me for a couple of seconds to check if I was fair dinkum. I kept up the façade for maximum effect. 'Mate, we can make these charges go away, don't worry about that,' he finally shot back at me.

And that was that. I was a free man … until the academy.

The idea of becoming a copper kind of grew on me again. Well, I guess under the circumstances it had to. Three months later, I'd passed the initial medical and psychology tests. I was called in and questioned on the psych component though.

One of the questions on the test was, 'Do you fear metal door handles in hospitals?' I told the truth. 'Yes, I do fear metal door handles in hospitals.' What can I say? I hate germs. Especially super-deadly hospital germs. And I told them so. After the call back they passed me, but they probably thought my response was a bit weird. I just thought the question was weird.

The academy was the next stop. I wasn't the most disciplined soldier on parade, and my first day could quite easily have been my last. I rocked up in a singlet and pair of boardies, my trusty thongs shuffling underneath me. I was under the impression that the academy would smooth out the rough edges, especially the messy long hair I'd cultivated in the months beforehand. I figured it was a waste of money forking out for a haircut when the academy was prepared to foot the bill for a short back and sides. Seemed the logical thing to do at the time.

Not surprisingly, I was immediately ridiculed by the academy's instructors and my fellow recruits. I got the feeling that I was in for a long four months.

To a man, the drill instructors were a bunch of pricks. They took it upon themselves to totally belittle and demoralise the less athletic and quieter recruits. I'm still not sure why they employed this tactic. Did they think they could turn us all into tough and rugged operators who could run a few Ks in ten minutes? Jesus, half the police force can't even walk 400 metres unless there's a pie at the end of the rainbow.

Thankfully I was on top of the physical and academic side of the program, but I was always landing myself in trouble for one thing or another. If it wasn't the length of my hair, it was the condition of my room. If it wasn't for being late to class, it was for being a smartarse when I was there. I couldn't wait till the weekend for a chance to get away from all the rules.

Four weeks into the course, I was close to going home for good. It all started when I was woken up at 6 a.m. for assembly. I was a bit tired and irritable after a few drinks at the local pub the night before. My duty that morning was to pick up cigarette butts from the academy's stairwell. I made an executive decision to go back to bed, and someone from the squad dobbed me in.

When I was called out, I told the drill instructor that I'd prefer to pick up the butts before I went to bed. You know, get an extra lie-in. Made sense to me. Well, you'd have thought that I'd just slept with his wife and eaten his dog for breakfast. After ten minutes of him carrying on and screaming in my face at close quarters I was handed another incident report, probably my third at that stage. I was told that if there was one more report, I'd be turfed out on my ear.

The very next day I managed to get another one, this time for hiding in a ditch during a cross-country run. It was a circuit course, and the plan was to rejoin the group on the final leg. I thought I'd timed it perfectly, even coming in second. Didn't want to make it too obvious, even though I looked remarkably fresh.

Again someone from the squad put me in, but I denied it. The sergeant who wrote up the report laughed at my denial. In the end, he even congratulated me on my initiative. For some reason, I was never kicked out.

The only part of academy life I enjoyed was the canteen food. I saw no point in not eating well. I'd be up and down for thirds and fourths at mealtime, flirting with the old ladies behind the counter. They were only too happy to help out their best customer.

At the same time, my roommate wanted out. Not out of the academy, but out of our room. He told an instructor that I would hide my mess in a cupboard before inspections. He just had to get it off his chest. Was there another recruit he could bunk down with who wasn't a lazy prick come inspection time, sir?

The days went so slowly, and graduation couldn't come fast enough. I ranked second out of thirty in my squad. I don't know who was more surprised, me or the instructors.

My first stop after the academy was Reservoir, a suburb in Melbourne's north. It was a shock at first. The crooks were scum, *real* Reservoir dogs. I couldn't understand their way of thinking at all. They were just pieces of shit — shitmen. And they were treated with the disrespect they deserved.

My stint at Reservoir was also back in the days of touch-typing. There were no tape recorders during interviews, and after you typed one page the crook was usually asleep from boredom. At the end of it all, no one could be bothered reading ten pages of police speak and they'd sign their lives away, case closed.

I was at Reservoir for about a year, then it was headquarters: Russell Street. I spent a lot of time on the State Parliament steps. That's where coppers with discipline problems hang out. Say hello to them next time you're there. They're nice people.

Although I did spend a disproportionate amount of my time patrolling the Spring Street steps, I wasn't a bad copper. I'd say I was just misguided, and I grew bored way too easily. When I was told to do something I had every intention of doing it, but I'd get pulled in a different direction, and before I knew it I was sidetracked again. I guess my real problem was that I found it difficult to take the job too seriously.

I liked the camaraderie of the force though. Coppers would all stick by each other. If you had a problem, it would be solved ... one way or another.

After Russell Street I landed at the call centre, D24. My job was to answer phones, collect the information, and then pass on the details to the units in the field. In a way I suppose it was like administering triage in a hospital's emergency ward. You had to judge the severity of a crime, and act upon it appropriately. For example, the policeman with a gunshot wound in Preston would be treated with far more urgency than the cat up the tree in Camberwell.

The discipline of the place was probably good for me too. D24 had a real in-your-face command structure. Young coppers often did a stint there, and we were too green to question much of anything. Our superiors (who probably would've preferred to be elsewhere too) were straight down the line, and for six months I played the game, and kept my nose clean, before being transferred to Box Hill in Melbourne's leafy east.

You'll find doors eventually open in the police force if you're not a complete idiot, so I was recommended for a secondment to the Drug Squad in 1990. It was more of a familiarisation exercise than anything else. I just felt that I'd get to play with the big boys for a few months, and then they'd send me back into uniform again.

Eight of us rolled up to the course. There was nothing special about the group whatsoever. We knew next to nothing about undercover work, or drugs for that matter. I was no angel growing up, but drugs were something foreign to me. I knew the basics, but I'd never even smoked a joint.

On the first day, one of the Drug Squad's undercovers spoke to us. Marty looked like one of those bikie scrotes with tatts all over him. He talked about guns, he talked about drugs, and I was thinking, 'Holy fuck!' I figured that I didn't have the balls to carry it off. People always thought I was overconfident, but the truth is I was shockingly shy. It was excruciating to watch sometimes too. As an example: if I walked into a shop without knowing if they sold a certain item, I'd have been unable to ask for it. It was just a fear of looking silly in front of people I didn't know. I'm a lot better now, but back then my mouth would go dry, my eyes would redden, and my palms would sweat up. No one knew this though. Years of practice ensured it was pretty well hidden.

Anyway, after Marty had finished his lecture he pulled me to one side. 'So, what do you think?'

'Fucken out of control,' I answered. And it was.

'Are you interested in doing undercover work yourself?'

'I'm not sure. I don't think I'd be able to pull it off.' My hands were sweating just talking to the bloke.

'Give it some thought. I reckon you'd be good at it.'

In all honesty the idea excited me, but I just couldn't picture myself fitting into the role of a seasoned criminal. Working undercover, I knew it would be a lot more difficult dealing with crooks when no other cops were in the vicinity. It's just like bikies. One of them is an unemployed bearded bloke with a Harley-Davidson. But when half a dozen of his mates are standing behind him twirling crowbars, his underpants are suddenly worn on the outside. There's a reason cops go out in pairs. We twirl batons though.

Being so young, I was also concerned that crooks wouldn't take me seriously. Plus, I didn't know their capabilities. Probably didn't know my own either.

Working for the Drug Squad at their headquarters was another matter entirely. That I could handle. It was a relaxed atmosphere, not so accountable, chilled out, wear what you want, whatever. My worry was the undercover component — but I didn't have to deal with that yet.

Undercover

After the secondment, life slipped back into the drudgery of wearing blue at Box Hill again. Next thing, though, I was taking a phone call from the Drug Squad. A position had come up, but not as a covert operative. And even though I was young, they wanted me.

Once I was with the Drug Squad, they were always at me to give undercover work a go. I was then informed, no, more like ordered, that the next course required my attendance. The bosses wanted me to do it. Resistance was futile.

Looking back, there was no need to worry. I was hesitant at first because of the shyness thing, but right from the first exercise, I enjoyed myself. The manipulation, the negotiations ... it all just started to become really natural.

The *Crimes Act* (an official document I had to sign before I attended the course) prevents me from going into a whole lot of detail, but you'd be thrust into situations where anything could happen. Most people froze or crapped themselves. Some people reached for their guns when the blowtorch was applied, just like a good police officer's trained to do. Others just kind of fell apart in front of you, unable to keep up the charade. They were simple exercises, but it exposed people. It really gave a glimpse into what sort of person you were.

I felt like I was in my element though. Under pressure, I didn't resort to the copper mentality. I enjoyed the role-playing and, unlike most of the others, I knew I had some control over it.

Other field exercises were interesting too. I remember being dropped off at a bikie pub, this pretty blond boy chucked in among the great unwashed. I thought the instructors had done it on purpose — so I'd get my head kicked in. I was such a headstrong little turd back then.

Damian Marrett

The idea was to circulate around the pub, meeting and greeting. There were conditions attached. Conversations with one person could not exceed fifteen minutes, and a drink limit was also imposed — just the one per hour ... That directive wasn't so strictly enforced.

I was there for three hours, drinking, talking, playing pool. In the corner, watching my every move, another 'patron' was assessing my performance. I was eager to show my wares. Without it being a requirement, I even recall asking a bikie where I could get on. I was probably a little premature — he told me I was in the wrong place.

At the debriefing, we had to give a description of what happened. I didn't take it too seriously. 'It was terrible. I walked in, and two bikies threw me up on the bar and fucked me up the arse!' I cried.

I got a few laughs, but not from the Inspector. Afterwards he summoned me to an audience and, not for the first time, threatened to kick me off the course. I'd received the same warning a couple of days before for excessive drinking after hours. Thankfully, a few of the working undercovers came to my rescue, and the Inspector had to wait for another slip-up.

The field exercises helped a lot with my self-esteem. Even though I came off like a joker who couldn't give a shit, I truly wanted to be the best. At the debriefings, my stories were easily the most outlandish. I loved using my imagination, and my confidence was sky-high.

As a result of my performances, I was starting to get positive feedback which indicated that my ability to think quickly on my feet was a real plus. I was also told that I didn't have any noticeable police mannerisms, and that I transcended the stereotypes. I didn't look like a cop — I was young and preferred to wear my hair long. I didn't talk

Undercover

like a cop. In fact, I'd always resisted that annoying official way that coppers speak, preferring to talk to people on their own level. And I certainly never acted like a cop, refusing to take myself too seriously.

I felt like I was going places by keeping it simple. Some people get the wrong idea about the way undercovers operate on a job. They think you've got to talk the talk, walk the walk, all that crap. But you don't have to come across as this big gangster to get results; things run a lot smoother when you just be yourself. Put it this way: good crooks don't tell other crooks they just shot someone unless they can get some mileage out of it. Good crooks keep you guessing. It's just like the mate who goes into detail about every root he's ever had. A dickhead's a dickhead, no matter what your line of work. Switched-on people can see through bullshit.

Anyway, I found that the exercises became easy for me because I could convince myself that I *was* the person I was playing. So if the exercise demanded that I was a heroin user, I was a heroin user; all I wanted was heroin. If the person in front of me had the heroin, I would never get angry with him. He had the power to tell me to piss off. I had to keep chipping away at him. If I kept at him, invariably I would get the heroin.

Of course there are specific ways you can calm a situation, divert suspicion, pull at people's heartstrings, be forceful, but they're all just smaller pieces in a bigger puzzle. When you put them all together and think on your toes, undercover work has a certain rhythm to it. Everything falls into place. At least, that's how it felt for me.

After the course, I was assessed on my performance. I was told all the basic things — 'quick on your feet, confident, have potential but you're still young'. People who weren't much chop were recommended for short-

Damian Marrett

term jobs or one-off buys. I was told that I'd be ideal for medium- to long-term jobs.

But even though the assessment was positive, I wasn't happy. All of those nice things to say and they came back with medium-term jobs. Well, that's all I could see at the time.

In hindsight, they probably thought I was a little prima donna, and didn't want to build me up too much. I loved a drink and a laugh, so on the surface I probably looked like a young bloke out for a good time, nothing more. Maybe they thought that, being so young, I'd struggle with the complexities of the work.

All I knew was that I was ready to go. I just needed something to cut my teeth on.

Two

May 23-24, 1992

In many ways, your garden-variety crooks are no different to the rest of us. Some are hard, some are soft, some are clever, and some are also brainless dumb-fucks. Patty Condro fit neatly into that last category. The bloke was no criminal mastermind; just the one phone call on Saturday May 23, 1992 confirmed this.

'G'day, is that Patty?'

'Yeah, who's this?' he fired back in a nasally whine that gave me the shits right from the get-go. When a supposedly hard bastard talks like Jeff Fenech on helium, it's pretty difficult to take said supposedly hard bastard seriously. Months later, transcribing hours of intercepts and wires featuring Patty and his talking nose, I was just about ready to chuck in the job.

'My name's Damian. I'm a mate of Barry's. Did he talk to you about me?'

'Nah.'

'Well, he was supposed to.'

'Mate, I don't even know any Barry.'

Shit, now *I* was the dumb-fuck. Barry, police informer C7/92, was in our keep. A pain-in-the-arse big-noter, he'd been busted for drug-related offences by the Swan Hill police. Consequently, Barry was prepared to assist us with information about drug dealer Patty Condro — if we were prepared to give him the thumbs up when the judge was fixing a sentence.

I'd actually put off making this phone call to Patty for over a week; blame my shyness for that one. My boss, Detective Sergeant Greg 'Googa' Hewitt, started getting suss when I kept telling him that Patty wasn't answering my calls. He mentioned giving Barry a bell, and tracking down Patty. Googa had forced my hand, so I reached for the phone.

But I hated cold starts. Most undercover jobs involved a personal introduction from an informer. I liked it that way. But sometimes first contact with a target required you to bump into them in a pub or just ring them up out of the blue. We called it a cold start, and I never could get used to them. I'd be crap at telesales.

'I'm after some green,' I ploughed on regardless. 'The bloke you don't know, Barry, gave me your number.'

Something twigged. Small, rusty cogs turned over upstairs. 'How much ya want?'

'Five pounds.'

'Yeah, that's no problem. Where ya from?'

'Melbourne. Can you bring it down here?' Patty lived in Swan Hill, an eight-hour round trip away. This appeared to be a smallish job, and it'd save a lot of time if he made the journey down the highway himself. Worth a try at least.

'Nah, you've gotta come up here.'

'Rightio. When can you have it ready?'

'Whenever.'

'How much?' I asked.

'Each one is $4500.'

'You can't go any lower?'

'Er ... $4400, but that's it,' he replied.

'Okay, yeah, okay. Five at $4400 then,' I said. No point in stretching out negotiations over the phone.

'Yeah. How much is that?'

'Twenty-two,' I said, doing the sums for him.

'Yeah, thanks. That's right.'

'I'll come up your way tomorrow then. I'll give you a call in the morning.'

'No worries.'

And that was it. We were off and running.

The job was coined Operation Bert. Bert and Patti Newton. Patty Condro. Hours of police manpower came up with that one. Or about two seconds of thought time by an offsider, Phil Strawhorn.

This wasn't my first undercover job, but I was still naive, even overwhelmed. Less than a year ago, I had been a uniformed copper working within the confines of strict behavioural guidelines. Now I was a covert operative mixing with criminals who liked to play it fast and loose.

Suddenly I'd become the centre of attention. It was like I'd gone from being an actor with just a late-night commercial under his belt to the genuine, bona fide star of the show. I was the centrepiece. Other coppers were always buzzing around me — and I must admit, I liked it.

In the months beforehand I'd been involved in a few operations that were yet to run their course, but it was no secret around the office that I was after bigger and better challenges. This early on in the piece, I wasn't sure where Patty Condro and his five pounds of grass would take me, but you never know your luck — the smallest lead can sometimes find you in the least likely places.

The next morning the crew set off in two vehicles, one a standard unmarked Crime Squad number, the other a hire car. The Drug Squad would often use rental cars. All crooks used them in those days because it was so easy to bodge your details during the hiring process. It was also extra insurance for us if the crooks checked our plates — the car could only be traced back to a rental place under a false name.

Five of us were included in the trip. Googa was my controller, a true professional, very thorough in his preparation. Lordy was the money man. His priority was a backpack stashed with twenty-two grand in cash. There was Rids, a glass-half-empty sort of guy who was convinced the whole operation would amount to nothing. And then Phil, a bloke who always played it for laughs: 'Hey, at least we get a night away on the Murray River. And if you do fuck it up, Damian, we'll all have something to laugh about on the drive back.'

Like many long car rides, most of the conversation was used up in the first hour. During the extended silences, I felt uncertain about the whole operation. The phone call to Patty Condro had been just too good to be true, and I didn't want to come out of the job looking like a dickhead.

The Drug Squad was a funny place: reputations were always on the line. Some undercovers were never even utilised just because of a perception that they couldn't cut it. If nothing else, I was determined that I'd never be in that position. My ego wouldn't allow it. There was no way I'd sit on my backside all day, simply because some self-appointed critic couldn't trust me to get it right.

Mid-morning I gave Patty a call on my mobile phone. This one was the size of a small TV set. We're talking vintage 1992. It weighed half a tonne when you carried it from place to place but, even so, crooks were always impressed when you lugged the clunky fucker around. In the early nineties drug dealers would crap on more about their mobiles than who won the footy on the weekend.

Undercover

This particular unit was Drug Squad–owned, but some of the snappier models (the weight of one brick, not two) were hired at $20 a day. When you had a hired one in your possession, it was always a case of 'get the job over quickly, and bring me back that bloody phone'. And if you called up a mate, it was close to a sackable offence. Patty Condro, however, was no mate.

'G'day Patty, it's Damian.'

'Yeah, yeah, Damian. Are you on your way up?'

'Yeah. Everything's set. Bloody cold, isn't it? Cold up there?'

'Um, yeah, cold up here too.'

'I should be there in an hour or so. Where do you want to meet?'

'Um, Riverside Park. It's in Swan Hill. Got a map on ya?' Patty asked.

'Yeah, I'll find it. Riverside Park. Next to the river, yeah?'

'How'd you know that?'

More evidence that we weren't dealing with a prodigious intellect. I waited a moment before replying to his question, expecting him to catch on. I was still waiting three or four seconds later.

'Just the name of the park, mate,' I replied.

'Huh?'

'Riverside, side of the river.'

'Oh yeah,' he said. 'Mate, you couldn't do us a favour and grab us half a dozen stubbies on the way through, could ya? I haven't got a car.'

Weird. 'Er, I s'pose so. Look, I'll call you when I get up there, okay?' I then hung up on my possible new drinking partner.

Next came Googa's briefing. I was given five specific instructions:

Damian Marrett

1. Don't leave the purchase site.
2. Hold onto the money until we have the grass.
3. Try to encourage bigger deals with the target.
4. If possible, identify Patty's supplier.
5. And Damian, whatever you do, don't lose the twenty-two grand.

At around two o'clock I strapped a tape recorder to my torso, and the microphones to my chest. I later grew to detest this routine. Not because of a concern that crooks would pat me down, more the fact that, down the track, my body reacted violently to this procedure. Duct tape and sweaty skin is a volatile combination; my chest was always covered in rashes and welts.

I then dropped Lordy and the money off at the Lake Boga car park, about ten minutes' drive south of Swan Hill. This is where we wanted the deal to go down after the initial meeting at Riverside Park. But really it was a car park only in name. A nondescript gravel affair beside the Murray Valley Highway, it probably didn't see much action. If you were driving past in May, you wouldn't even give the joint a second glance. A couple of picnic tables sat miserably next to an unspectacular expanse of lake with only the hum of the semitrailers hurtling down the highway to keep them company. And that was about the sum total of it. Although I think the Lake Boga Tourist Board wished the lake was bluer.

When I pulled out of the car park Lordy was standing by the water's edge necking a VB. One of Patty's beers had already been taxed. Should've bought Lordy a coffee instead. Poor bloke was freezing out there.

During the drive to meet Patty I switched on the recording device, the on/off switch conveniently located in my jeans pocket.

Undercover

'Today is the 24th of May, 1992, and the day is Sunday. This is Detective Senior Constable Damian Marrett attached to the Drug Squad. I'm working in an undercover capacity in relation to Operation Bert. The time is now 2:18 p.m. I'm currently en route to the Riverside Park car park in Swan Hill where I'll be meeting target Patty Condro.

'The meeting was chosen and requested by the target three hours earlier when I called him on the telephone. He should have five pounds of cannabis for which I have told him that I will pay twenty-two thousand dollars.

'Detective Senior Constable Lord is at the Lake Boga car park with the money. This is where the exchange will be conducted. I've just parked in the Riverside Park car park now, so I'll stop the tape here and recommence it on the arrival of the target.'

At Riverside Park I gave Patty a reminder call. He was ready, so I described the car to him and waited. Perched beside the Murray River, it was a pleasant enough delay, with willows and gums providing a shady haven on the Victorian side of the border. Could've cracked open a stubbie and watched the world go by myself.

Recording device activated again: 'Tape recommenced at 2:52 p.m. Target approaching.'

A confused-looking Patty wandered into the car park. I stepped out of the car, and even though I seemed to be the only person within a 10 km radius, I shot him a confused look back. Didn't want to appear too chummy, even though I'd seen his photo on our profile.

'Patty?'

'Yeah. G'day, Damian.' Patty's mitt swallowed my hand in one. I sized him up — and there was a lot of size to size up. Patrizio (Patty) Condro was a seriously big bloke. In years gone by he'd apparently made his living as a standover man and small-time drug dealer in Melbourne's northern suburbs. In his early thirties, he'd recently moved back to family in Swan Hill, continuing to deal drugs in order to support his heroin habit.

For all his flaws — a heroin addiction being the major one — Patty was still a big bloke with a nasty reputation. And there's always a chance that big blokes can turn nasty, even when they come across like a playful puppy that talks out of its nose. Maybe he was like a dumb dog trained the wrong way. One stuff-up and a little bloke like me could be on the end of a mauling.

'You're very big.' I thought I'd state the obvious to kick off proceedings.

He looked at me strangely. 'Yeah.'

I should also add that Patty Condro was no catwalk model. To be honest, he was a big, fat, smelly, ugly bastard with a long, greasy poodle mullet — standard poodle, not a toy one. Under Patty's sizeable conk was an unkempt handlebar mo that required urgent attention on the trimming front. His clothes were straight off the Salvos' half-price rack. Or maybe his mum did his shopping for him. Either way, I never saw him in anything more polished than a pair of trackydacks and an old flannelette shirt two sizes too small for his frame. Mind you, I wasn't a card-carrying member of the style police myself, decked out in a T-shirt, flannelette, jeans and desert boots. But I was meant to look like a layabout surfie dude. It was my job. Patty just looked dirty.

'Got those stubbies?' he asked, a man-size thirst on his mind.

'Yeah, helped myself to one on the way through, though.' I grabbed the VBs from the front seat, and handed them over. Patty Condro: one beer short of a six-pack.

'No worries. How much do I owe ya?'

'Don't worry about it.'

'Thanks mate,' he said, twisting the top off one. 'So ya still want five?' He was talking pounds of grass now, not stubbies of VB.

'Yeah, five this time, but I want it to keep going. If you turn out to be fair dinkum, there could be some big stuff down the track.'

'Yeah, like what?' Patty instantly brightened up. It was as easy as that. Before I talked volume, he'd been less than enthusiastic. Different story now. Thought he might land a big one, or the scraps off a big one, more likely. Even at this early stage it was plain to see that Patty was just the middleman between supplier and buyer. He'd probably get a few hundred bucks as a kickback for introducing this deal.

'Don't worry. We'll talk about that later,' I replied. 'Let's just see how the first one goes, hey.'

Most undercover drug jobs run in a similar fashion. You go and buy a taste. If the sample's good, you buy some more. If everything goes according to plan, you then push them for the big one. That's how real drug transactions occur naturally anyway. It's not exactly rocket surgery or, er, brain science, if you know what I mean. This was the plan with Patty. Just establish trust and get him interested. After some of the smaller deals went smoothly, hopefully his suppliers would take an interest as well. When everyone's on for the ride, that's when you set up a killer deal for the buy/bust. I guess that was my job in a nutshell.

'How do you know Barry?' he quizzed me.

I spun some bullshit story about fixing our informer up with some smack through a mate of mine in Melbourne. He fired a few more questions at me, but gave the impression that he didn't really care about the answers too much. Just following orders from higher up.

'Barry gives me the shits anyway,' I said. 'Don't want much to do with the prick.' I mean, seriously, no one could've actually liked the scumbag. Also, informers are good for introductions, but any presence afterwards can run you into trouble. An early objective in most undercover operations is to remove the gig (our name for an informer), even from conversation, otherwise the dickheads will find ways to stuff it up for you every time. Once you get rid of them, everything that comes out of your mouth should be spot on.

'Yeah, yeah, he's a dickhead.' I got the feeling that Patty did a lot of agreeing.

'Okay, my mate's holding the money down at the lake,' I said. 'Now if anything goes wrong, you won't see us again.'

He fired a shocked look at me that was supposed to say, 'Nothing will go wrong, trust me'. In reality, he just looked fat and stupid.

'All right then, where's the gear at?' I asked.

'You'll have to drive me to get it. Let's get the money first.'

'Nah, the money's not going anywhere. Look, I don't know you from a bar of soap. Bring the gear, you get the money. That's how it works, Patty.' I was firm on this one. Don't leave the purchase site. Googa would be proud of me.

'How about you ring my mate then?' he asked, pointing at my mobile phone.

'No chance. Battery's dead. How about you come and have a look at the money, and then we'll drive to . . . ?'

'Um, Vince's.'

'Yeah, we'll go to Vince's house and look at the gear.' I knew that I was now going against a directive, leaving the purchase site and meeting with this bloke Vince. Maybe Googa wouldn't be so proud of me now, but I weighed it

Undercover

up against another one of his directives: make inroads into identifying the supplier. This buy was going places. I'd be crazy not to follow through on an invitation to visit Patty's supplier.

'Yeah, okay, that sounds good,' Patty said. I was a bit shocked that he agreed to that one. Usually a go-between like Patty would throw a few extra dollars onto the asking price without the supplier's knowledge. He did seem to be the agreeable type though. Mind you, I was still worried that things appeared a little too easy, and that he may have been planning to rip us off. But one look at him in his blue tracksuit pants with his pathetic guts spilling out and the fear subsided. I mean, the only person who could've possibly feared Patty Condro was the proprietor of the local all-you-can-eat joint. And there was no way a gun could be concealed down those pants. Maybe in his rolls of fat, but not in his pants. Besides, Lordy was armed. I felt safe.

So, it was back to a frozen Lordy on the shores of Lake Boga, an 'aquatic playground', so the sign said. Not much playground activity on the cusp of winter, however.

Lordy opened up the backpack and Patty stuck his head in for a close-up. I explained to Lordy that we were going to Vince's place to check out the grass, and then we'd come back and hand over the money. He told us to hurry. 'Mate, it's bloody cold down here.' Yeah, yeah.

I was starting to enjoy myself. Everything was running smoothly, so it was off to meet Vince at a house in Ridge Road, Tresco. Another five minutes further south from Swan Hill, Tresco is an Italian fruit-growing area, orchards on both sides of the road. There's a sign saying, 'Welcome to Tresco'; 100 metres later it's only a memory. You've seen the lot: no pub, no shop, nothing. You don't even have to slow down from 100 kmh.

Damian Marrett

We pulled up to a weatherboard shack to be greeted by an overdressed Italian bloke in his thirties. His *Miami Vice*–style clobber didn't quite match the house he'd just exited from. Hello Vince.

It was a Sunday afternoon, but Vince was wearing a shiny silver suit with a crisp white shirt underneath. Frankly the whole outfit looked ridiculous, particularly when it was stacked up against our flannelette.

It was only later that the Drug Squad discovered that Vince was actually Matteo Rosario Medici, or Matt to his drug-dealing mates. Hailing from Mildura, a town about two hours upriver from Swan Hill, Medici was using his brother Vince's name for reasons known only to himself.

Medici was a local drug dealer and standover merchant with a fearsome reputation. Whenever you mentioned his name to local coppers, they'd pretty much say the same thing: 'That fucking prick. We want to get that bastard.' We were clearly not dealing with a Renaissance man in Medici. We were dealing with a total scumbag, a fact his own father found out too late.

When the old man upset local Mafioso colleagues, apparently the whole of the Medici family had been placed in the firing line — standard operating procedure for the Mafia. Medici Jr took a pretty drastic course of action to remedy the situation: he blew his dad's head off with a shotgun. The killing of his father saved the family from future mob reprisals, and gave Matteo an instant reputation as a bloke not to be messed with.

Medici was later acquitted of murder, coughing up a sob story about the regular beatings his family had endured over the years, courtesy of his old man. At the hearing, Medici's legal team claimed their client had an IQ of 76. Any score below 75 and you're well on your way to mental retardation. The judge took pity on Matt Medici the borderline imbecile, and he escaped any real jail time.

His indiscretions didn't stop there. In November 1988 Medici and his mother were both convicted of trafficking 93 kilos of cannabis, valued at half a million dollars. He was sentenced to four-and-a-half years, serving less than two years.

He was also the primary target of Operation Reuben, another Victoria Police Drug Squad initiative that was just winding down. Two undercovers had been flying into Mildura and picking up pounds of grass from him. They even gave him a Holden ute to stash full of grass for them.

Before things got too involved Medici's girlfriend got spooked, letting her boyfriend know that one of the undercovers looked like a Queensland copper she knew. She was wrong, but Medici didn't want to play any more. The ute was returned, no contraband inside.

Now that we'd arrived on the scene, Bert would kill off Reuben. By no means was it a fair fight: Medici was 100 per cent sold on his girlfriend's story that he was being set up. Reuben was going nowhere.

But all of those Medici facts were revealed to me after that first meeting. Now I was standing in a Tresco front yard buying drugs off a couple of Italians, one whose fashion plate had been smashed years beforehand.

'Vince, this is the bloke I was telling you about,' said Patty, shuffling out of our way. He was clearly intimidated. And I suspected it wasn't because of Medici's superior fashion sense.

'G'day, I'm Damian. Just knock off work?' I asked, referring to the choice of threads. Who knows? Maybe he'd just got back from church.

'Work? I don't work,' he spat out. 'I always look good.'

'Nice suit,' I lied.

He just nodded. 'Where's the money?'

Before I could answer, Patty pulled him to one side, bringing him up to speed on the deal's progress. It didn't go down too well. 'You were supposed to bring the money here, you dumb shit!' Medici shouted, thrashing his arms just inches from poor Patty's ears. 'It was simple, and you fucked it up.' Patty's eyes were fixed to the ground, too scared to make any move. Medici took this as his cue to pace the front yard. We had a live one on our hands here.

'Mate, what's the problem?' I chipped in. 'Patty's seen the money. Let's just get in the car and do the deal.'

Medici's head rocked from side to side, processing this new information. It was like his whole world had just caved in. Secretly, I was enjoying this little performance piece on the front lawn. It was giving me a good understanding of the way the bloke operated. Matt 'Vince' Medici was all ego.

'Is this where you tell me that you had problems getting that much gear?' I was such a little smartarse.

Well, that was it. I'd set him off big time. 'Do you fucken know who I am? This is chicken shit to me. Five fucken pounds!' he roared, ego out of its box. 'Yeah, I've got the fucken gear. Shit, I just didn't want to drive anywhere for a chicken-shit five pounds. Jump in your car and I'll follow you down. Five fucken pounds. And you're a dumb shit, Patty.'

'Let's just do it,' I said. 'Then everyone's happy.'

'Nah mate, it's not your fault. We'll do this thing now,' he said, his eyes following Patty waddling his way to my car before invitations had been sent out. I jumped back in behind the wheel. After the little altercation in the front yard, Patty was grateful to be my navigator again. Medici followed us in a silver Ford Fairlane, same colour as his suit.

'Maybe you should look at getting yourself a suit like Vince's,' I joked to Patty, chucking a U-ey out of the driveway. 'He looks smooth.'

He laughed. I don't think he was used to people taking the piss out of Medici. Probably enjoyed it. But even so, Patty Condro knew his place.

'Mate, ya can't fuck this bloke round. He's done some pretty bad things,' he said.

'Yeah?'

'All I'm saying is don't fuck him round. Okay?'

'How come?'

Patty paused, unsure if he should continue. 'He shot his old man.'

'What? Killed him?'

'Yeah. Shot him in the head. With a shotgun.'

'Fair dinkum?'

'Yeah, ya don't wanna fuck with him, Damian.'

'Rightio mate. I understand,' I said. 'Pass us that piece of paper, will you, Patty? I'll give you my phone number. And the pager too.' I wrote them down, steering the car at the same time. Patty was busy disguising a smile, just thrilled to be a part of the action. 'Yeah, give me a call if you don't hear from me for a while,' I said. 'You know, just in case I can't get hold of you.'

'I'm usually home, but thanks mate,' he replied, stuffing the numbers into his wallet.

'No worries.'

'Just one thing. Make sure Vince doesn't cut me out, hey, Damian. Tell him you want me here all the time.'

'Don't worry, mate. I'll look after you.'

Moments later we pulled up at Lake Boga. The wind coming off the water was as Antarctic as it ever gets in northwest Victoria. I even felt a hint of compassion for the brave soldier Lordy when I introduced him to Medici.

'Lordy, this is Vince.'

'Hey, nice suit, mate,' he said. Medici's choice of clobber was proving to be a great little conversation starter.

Medici just grunted. 'You got the money?'

'Yeah. You seen the grass, Dame?' Lordy asked.

Before I had a chance to answer, Medici told us to get into the back seat of his car so he could show us the gear. All three of us and the backpack of cash climbed into Medici's Fairlane. It was a tight squeeze with Patty beaching himself in the thick of it — no chance the fat oaf was going to be cut out of this deal.

Medici walked over to the boot of the car, and I suddenly felt exposed. Three bunnies in the back seat, and a bloke behind the car we couldn't see. A bloke who had killed his old man.

I looked over at Lordy. He didn't look concerned, but he also didn't know the details of the 'Vince Shoots Father Through Head with Shotgun' story. I looked over my shoulder without trying to raise any suspicion. Through the back windscreen, a small crack in the raised boot gave me a reasonable line of sight.

I could make out Medici fumbling around. He then removed two black garbage bags. Things looked good. He waltzed over to the back seat, flinging the gear at us. I took a look inside both bags. Lordy and I agreed that it appeared to be cannabis, and it appeared to weigh about five pounds.

Lordy opened up his backpack as we all poured out of the car, two relieved coppers happy to breathe again. 'There's twenty grand in fifties, and the rest is in hundreds,' he said.

'No worries,' Medici said, throwing the bag in the boot. He didn't even bother counting it out, but you could tell his load had been lightened. I think I even detected a smile. In turn, Lordy turfed the bags of grass into our car.

Drug-dealing etiquette suggests that you get moving once money and gear are exchanged, but there were a few more formalities that needed addressing.

'I was saying to Patty that we'd be interested in keeping things going,' I said.

'Yeah? What do you want?' asked Medici.

'What have you got?'

'Well, whaddya fucken want?' Medici's anger switch was perilously close to the *on* position again.

'I'm after powders,' I blurted out.

'Yeah, I can get fucken powders. You want yogi?'

Yogi? What in the fuck was yogi? Going by Medici's personality, speed. Going by his suit, cocaine. 'Yeah, can you get us a sample?'

'For when?'

'I'll ring Patty tomorrow.'

'How much will you want?' Medici asked.

'Just an ounce to start with. If the green goes well, we'll be up for more of that too,' I said. 'Can you keep that going as well?'

'Can I fucken keep it going? Yeah, I can keep it going.'

Medici was proving to be a major pain in the arse. 'I'll call Patty tomorrow, then,' I said.

'Look, it's bloody cold. I'm getting out of here,' Medici said, heading for the Fairlane. Patty tagged along, eagerly waiting for his cut.

Lordy and I jumped in the hire car and took off. It was time for some more wire-wearing legal requirements, and to provide a short synopsis of what had just taken place: 'Yeah, okay, the time is now 4:22 p.m. With me is Detective Senior Constable Lord. We're leaving the purchase site at Lake Boga after purchasing what appears to be five pounds of cannabis from target Patty Condro and a man identified only as Vince.

'We also had a discussion in relation to them providing us with a sample, an ounce, of what we believe is amphetamines, er, maybe cocaine. We also discussed future purchases of cannabis. I'll be calling the target tomorrow to discuss the situation further. In a short time I'll be meeting with Detective Sergeant Hewitt where I'll hand him over the green vegetable matter which I believe to be cannabis. So I'll stop the device here at about 4:23 p.m.'

Three

MAY 25–JUNE 5, 1992

Put very simply, surveillance is the method of tracking criminals' moves — hopefully without their knowledge. In a fashion, anti-surveillance is the opposite. Sometimes criminals were tracking *my* every move, hopefully *with* my knowledge.

You'd often find that good crooks worked their own surveillance networks. Some were very sophisticated in scope. On one operation, a target installed a listening device behind the minibar fridge in my motel room. It was quite an unnerving discovery, but understandable considering the circumstances. When there's so much at stake (on that particular job, millions of dollars worth of drugs), it makes perfect sense to protect your assets.

It also made perfect sense for me to search for, detect and then bin listening devices. Crooks are always paranoid about coppers, so if I was hunting around for any evidence of police presence, I was just doing what every good criminal does: making sure I didn't get caught.

Anti-surveillance isn't just limited to thinking like a crook. It also involves taking precautionary measures to avoid detection when driving a car. The idea is to make constant use of your rear-view mirror. Sometimes you stop in a driveway for no reason, checking if anyone takes an interest in your detour. You'd also whip into no-name back streets, waiting to see if anyone did the same. A fifteen-minute trip on the way to work could conceivably blow out to half an hour, even when no one was tailing me.

Despite all that, on the Monday morning drive to the office following the first Bert deal I gave no thought to the latest developments in anti-surveillance techniques. The crooks were safely tucked away in Swan Hill and Mildura with no reason to doubt my credentials as a fellow drug dealer.

At that time, head office was located inside two floors of the Russell Street complex in the heart of Melbourne's CBD. This area of the city also happened to be the epicentre of criminal presence in Victoria. Crooks were being arrested, and then hauled away to the Magistrates Court or watch-house over the road. Others were signing in on bail or just waiting for their mates to be released. If you were an undercover policeman, it was *the* most prominent place in the state to be detected. Kind of negated all the anti-surveillance hard yards you might have clocked on the way there.

Our two floors at Russell Street housed 100 or so Drug Squad employees in a space that, on reflection, was probably in need of one of those TV makeovers. Old and crumbly, grubby and grotty, it would've been state of the art back in the fifties.

My desk was easy to find. It was the one that looked like a bomb had gone off on top of it; paperwork was never my strongest suit. One morning I came into the office to discover some resident joker had cordoned off my work station with metres of crime scene tape.

One of the more interesting features of that particular office was located in a side corner. We called it the 'hello phone'. When we gave targets our contact details, they'd be given the hello phone number. You have to remember that this was before the mobile phone explosion.

Undercover

If you walked past the hello phone when it rang, strangely enough you answered with just the one word: *Hello*. If the call wasn't for you, you'd hunt down the other undercover it was for. A sign placed above the phone was a constant reminder to passing morons who might inadvertently give the game away. 'Good afternoon, this is Senior Detective Damian Marrett of the Victoria Police Drug Squad. How may I help you? Um, I mean, hello.'

I'd given Patty Condro the number for the hello phone, but I'd also told him that I'd make contact with him first. When I did so on Monday, his phone rang out twice.

Besides stringing along Patty and Matt Medici, I did have other concerns — yogi being one of them. What was it? I didn't want the whole Melbourne office to know that I was struggling with drug slang on one of my first jobs, so I reached for a glossary listing street terminology.

Yogi was sandwiched in there between *ying* (cannabis) and *yuppie flu* (the effects of a cocaine snorting habit). According to the experts, yogi was a street term for cocaine. I wasn't convinced. *Yo* rhymes with *go*, which is amphetamine, and despite the million dollar threads, Medici looked like a speed man to me.

Another concern was Operation Pawnbroker. My very first undercover job was set to run its course.

Pawnbroker was a funny one. I suppose you could have called it a test run to see if I could cope with the pressures of undercover work. If I didn't screw up, I'd probably be considered when better, more involved operations came down the line.

Pawnbroker's principal target, Sammy Cox, was a dumb-arse repeat offender from Preston. The bloke couldn't help himself getting into trouble. In his mid-twenties, he came from a family of about a dozen kids. Apparently some of the offspring didn't even know their dates of birth. Their mum just kept squeezing them out at home without bothering to jot down the details.

Early on, I offered Sammy some friendly advice: 'We've got to be careful, mate. We don't want coppers nosin' round.'

'Don't worry, I can smell coppers a mile away,' Sammy said, blowing smoke rings out his own backside. 'It's a special talent I've got.' Some talent. The stupid nuffy had been separately dealing drugs to five different undercovers for the last three months.

After letting some smaller deals run (a few grams of heroin here and there), buy/bust time had arrived. Sammy would sell me an ounce of heroin, and I'd hand over $8000. Bloody expensive, but heroin was at a premium in those days.

It was supposed to be a textbook transaction, but, not for the first time in the history of undercover work, things played out a little bit differently.

The purchase site was outside Circle K on Broadway in Reservoir. I was wired, and the local coppers were ready to intercept once we had the gear. It was a small job; no Special Operations Group ninjas to put the frighteners on Sammy after I gave the bust signal.

'Okay, how do you want to do this?' I asked, loitering in the car park with an edgy target.

'Give me the cash, and I'll get you the gear.'

'Nah. I want to see the gear first. Where is it?'

'Round the corner, down there,' he answered, pointing to a side street.

'Well, let's take a look at it, then.'

'Nah, this bloke won't do the deal if you get him involved.'

'Come on, Sammy. You know me.'
'Mate if it was up to me, no worries. But this guy ...'
'What about if I come with you, then?'
'Nup, he won't do that.'
'So you want me to just stand round here after giving you the eight grand? That's fucken bullshit, mate.'
'I know, I know.'

He appeared rock solid. I was wired, but it was only a taping device, so nobody could hear what was going on. There was a fair degree of surveillance though. I tossed up whether to hand over the money or fight it out. I knew that when Sammy moved, plenty of eyes would be moving with him, but I decided that it wasn't worth the risk.

'Nah, this is crap,' I said, standing my ground. 'If I don't see the drugs, you don't get the money.'

Sammy finally relented, leading me around the corner where a mate of his, Joey Schipano, was waiting. After introductions, the same bullshit conversation went round in circles again. He wanted the money before I saw the drugs.

Ten minutes later, I'd bored everyone senseless by refusing to budge. Sensing that his cut of the deal was on the line, Joey then pointed to a cigarette packet in the gutter. It was a common practice for drugs to be stooked (hidden) a short distance from the purchase site.

'It's in there,' Joey said.

I walked over to the crumpled pack of Winny Reds, picked it up and flipped it open. Inside was a small plastic bag full of white powder. I then took my cap off, a signal for the police bust team to move in. After a moment of fumbling around to buy the arresting police some time, I then handed the eight grand over to Joey.

We said our goodbyes, and then I watched as the two crooks waltzed off with the cash. This was wrong. No coppers were attached to their backs. Obviously the bust signal hadn't got through.

Unable to do much of anything, I raced back to my car and made for the rendezvous point. When I arrived there, I was informed that the situation was under control. Cox, Schipano and a third party, local hood Marco Grioli, had been arrested at the local TAB.

Surveillance had picked up the money being handed over from Schipano to Grioli. When the coppers jumped Grioli, the majority of the money was in his tracksuit pants (Schipano and Cox had already taken their cut). Later, the serial numbers matched the photocopies we'd taken of the cash before the bust. Pawnbroker was a success.

Months later, Cox copped a six-month stretch, Schipano one and a half, and supplier Grioli three years.

Feeling pretty pleased with myself, I drove back to the office and Operation Bert. On cue, my pager went off. Patty Condro was trying to track me down. Back at Russell Street I gave him a call.

'Patty, it's Damian. How's everything?'

'Good, good mate.'

'Everyone happy?'

'Yeah, no worries here.'

'And the other stuff we talked about?' I asked.

'Um, when do ya want it?'

'Soon. Probably Saturday.'

'Um, I'll have to check. Call me in a couple of days, could ya?' he asked.

'There's no problem, is there, Patty?'

'Nah, nah, should be right.'

'Vince's reliable, yeah?'

'Yeah, no worries on that one.'

'How much is it then?'

'Twelve hundred,' he replied.

Twelve hundred dollars an ounce: speed it was. I knew Medici's silver suit was all show.

'Okay. I'll also take two of what I got on Sunday as well. You know?'

'Yeah, yeah, I'll speak to Vince.'

'All right, I'll call you Wednesday. If you don't hear from me, you've still got my pager number, right?'

'Yeah, okay mate.'

Two days later, I called up Patty again. 'What's happening, mate?'

'You know, all right,' he said, not making any sense.

'Are we set for Saturday?'

'Um, what do you want again?'

'Fucken hell, Patty,' I said, more frustrated than angry. 'One of the yogi, and two of what we got Sunday.'

'Yeah, okay. I'll have to speak to Vince.'

'But you fucken said you'd talk to him the other day.'

'I did. Yeah, I'll just check again.'

'What the fuck's going on, Patty? Can you get Vince to ring me then?'

'Nah, he won't ring ya, Damian.'

'Have you fucken spoken to Vince or not?'

'Yeah, I've spoken to him,' said Patty.

'Well, what's the problem, then?'

'I've just gotta check with him again.'

'That's fine, Patty, but are we gonna do this thing or not?'

'Yeah, yeah, I'll call ya later today, okay?'

'Look, this isn't working, mate. Why don't you get Vince to ring me?' I asked.

'Nah, everything's all right. I'll call ya later, okay?'

'Fuck, Patty, there's gonna be some big stuff after this one, and I'm gonna look after you. You know that. Just put me onto Vince.'

'He won't call ya, I swear, Damian. Look, I'll call ya later.'

'Okay. What time?'

'In a couple of hours.'

Frustrating stuff. Shitkicker Patty was seemingly more worried about his cut than anything else.

The weekend came and went. Still no return call from Patty Condro. I gathered it was probably one of three things: Medici couldn't get the gear; Patty was screwing me around so that he had time to deal with Medici; or someone had heard something, and the deal was off. I was hoping it was number two.

I rang again first thing Monday, and there was no answer. Finally, Patty paged me at four in the afternoon. I called him the next day to teach the prick a lesson. Let him hang out for a while.

'Patty, it's Damian. What the fuck's going on?'

'G'day Damian. How are ya?'

'Fucken pissed off actually. I thought you were gonna call back.'

'Yeah, sorry about that.'

'What's the problem? My man's gettin' fucken annoyed.'

'I couldn't get hold of Vince. He lives in Mildura, you know.'

'I'll ring him then. Sort this shit out.'

'Nah, I'll call you this arvo. We'll be ready to go by then, I reckon.'

'Fucken hope so, Patty. Call me later.'

Around four o'clock, the hello phone went off. It was Patty with some news — finally, some good news. The deal

Undercover

was set for Friday at the Lake Boga car park. Two pounds of cannabis, one ounce of amphetamines. Operation Bert was gathering pace.

That night, we entertained some New South Wales undercovers at a restaurant in Lygon Street, Carlton, and then went on to the Chevron nightclub for some more bevvies. I couldn't believe the cars the Sydney undercovers had at their disposal. While we were running around town in ten-year-old shitboxes, these cowboys drove turbo-charged, late model Mazda RX7s with all the latest gadgets. James Bond to our Inspector Clouseau. Fucken show ponies.

After squeezing every last drop of hospitality out of my body, I got home at six the next morning, none too flash. At eight-thirty my phone rang at home. It was Inspector McCoy, my boss at the Drug Squad.

'Damian, you'd better get in here. One of the New South Wales cars was pinched from outside the Chevron last night.'

'Fucken hell. One of the RX7s?'

'Correct.'

'Shit. I'll be in soon.'

I took a quick shower, careful not to wake my housemate Nick, who preferred to sleep when it was light outside. When I walked to my car, I did a double take at what was sitting in my driveway: the bloody RX7. Shit. Must've pinched the keys off one of the Sydney boys and driven it home.

I went back inside and rang McCoy. 'Yeah boss, it's Damian. About that car . . .'

'Yes.'

'If I can find that car before lunchtime, any chance of a day off?'

'What do you know, Detective?'
'Well, it appears to be in my driveway, boss.'
'What?'
'Yeah, the thief must've driven it to my house.'
Short pause. 'I'll see you when you get in, Mr Marrett.'

On the drive to return the RX7, fragments of last night's fun and games popped into my mind. Yes, I had been in the 'stolen' car, but I recalled that Phil Strawhorn was the man behind the wheel. I took over after he had dropped himself off at his house, ten minutes away. I definitely wasn't the original culprit. Just thought I'd clear that up.

Half an hour later, I walked into McCoy's office and timidly handed over the keys. 'Great detective work, Mr Marrett,' he said, a dry smile on his face.

I was lucky McCoy had a sense of humour. Unlike the NSW undercover who spent a good ten minutes inspecting his 'stolen' vehicle upon its return.

Back in the office, I was acquainting myself with Matteo Medici's weighty police file. By this stage I was well aware of 'Vince' Medici's true identity and, flicking through his priors, he appeared to be a nasty work in progress.

Besides his obvious love affair with drug dealing — and his patricidal past — Medici was a well-rounded crook, exploring all the rich veins of criminal activity that life offered. This pony was quite the trickster. In 1989 he'd hoped to extort more than $23 000 a week from a number of Mildura businessmen. The classic standover tactic: if they didn't cough up the cash, he threatened them with violence. He was also picked up on police surveillance tapes discussing the kidnapping of a local businessman's son in return for a $10 million ransom.

Medici was sentenced to three years' jail on the

Undercover

blackmail charges, but thanks to the early release scheme he slipped back into his silver suit after serving only ten months, much to the chagrin of the local community.

Just browsing through his record, it was a miracle the bloke was a free man at all and, the truth be known, his file was a nightmare to follow. Medici had served so many concurrent sentences that a crack team of actuaries would've struggled to sort out when the prison gates were due to be unlocked.

Anyway, two days later, the same Drug Squad team of five was once again up Swan Hill way trying our luck with Australia's most fortunate crook. This time Lordy's backpack was stashed with ten grand — $8800 for the two pounds of grass and $1200 for the ounce of speed. When we pulled into the car park Medici's silver Fairlane was already there. He and another bloke were sitting in the front seat, Patty taking up the rear.

I activated the recording device before we hopped out of the car and approached on foot. Medici, taking a fashion risk with a teal double-breasted suit over a white T-shirt, wound down his window. 'Jump in the back with Patty, boys.'

Lordy and I did as requested, pushing Patty over into the corner. 'This is Neville,' Medici said.

The bloke behind the wheel turned around and nodded. His name was Neville Wise, a local drug-dealing nobody. A close associate of Medici's, Wise was the sort of bloke you wouldn't notice in a crowd. If people were colours, Medici was red, the colour of blood; Wise was beige, the colour of his hair.

'All set then, are we?' I asked, leaning forward with my arms resting on the front seat.

'Got the money?' Medici replied.

'Yeah,' Lordy said, tapping his backpack.

43

Damian Marrett

'We couldn't get the green,' said a gloomy Patty.

'How come?'

'Our bloke won't separate. He's selling fifty at a time,' said Medici.

'Fifty elbows?' I asked. An elbow is a pound.

'Yeah.'

'Mate, I wish I fucken had've known that,' I said, planting a seed. 'We wanted more anyway. That other stuff was good.'

Medici smiled. 'Always the best.'

'So you can't get us any green at all?'

'Not this time.'

'Any chance of more coming up soon?'

'A good chance, yeah, no problem,' said Medici.

'Yeah, but I want it cheaper next time round.'

'I'll see what I can do. I gotta make somethin' off it too, ya know.'

'What about the speed?' I asked. 'My man wants a shitload of that too.'

'It's twenty grand an elbow.'

'What's the quality like?'

'Mate, you'll love this stuff, guaranteed,' Medici said, puffing his chest out, rippling the lapels on his glossy teal ensemble.

'Let us have a think about it, but we want a heap of it. I'll get back to you on it, okay?'

I looked over at Patty. Unlike Medici, who was all front, Patty couldn't conceal his fear. The volumes had jumped a lot, and you could read his mind so easily. It went something like this: *Shit, am I getting in over my head? Who is this bloke? He's pretty young.*

'I'll call you about it soon, yeah,' I said once again to Medici.

Undercover

'Go through Patty. He'll sort it out,' he replied, his eyes peering over the top of his Ray-Bans. Sitting next to Lordy, Patty sat high in the saddle again, a toothy smile breaking out. He was a man who sorted things out.

'No problems,' I said.

'Let's do this deal then. I've got other shit to do.'

Medici handed me the speed sample, and I popped it into my pocket. Lordy rummaged around in his bag, counted out $1200 in notes, and handed them over to Medici in the front seat.

'I'm off then. Can you blokes drop Patty back home?' Medici asked.

We piled out of the car, and before we had a chance to answer the Fairlane was out of there, spitting dust behind it. I turned to Patty, who was looking south, shuffling his shoes in the gravel. 'Lordy, wait here, could ya? I'm gonna drop Patty off.'

To be honest, I was happy to share a bit of time with Patty, so we both jumped in the Commodore for the five-minute drive to Tresco.

'Are you sure Vince can deliver a lot of speed?' I asked him.

'Yeah, he knows what he's doing.'

'He's not bullshitting me?'

'Nah, he knows his stuff, Damian.'

'It's just that he comes across as this big man.'

'He'll back it up.'

'It's not just me who wants this gear, you know. There's other people.'

'Yeah I know,' he said. 'It sounds like you'll be wanting a lot of gear.'

'It's not all for me, you know.'

'Who's it for?' Patty couldn't help himself.

Damian Marrett

I didn't mind helping him out. Patty Condro was a pretty simple bloke. When you started talking about large amounts of drugs (coupled with large amounts of jail time), a fellow like Patty wanted reassurance and protection. Someone important on his side.

'Most of it's going through my uncle,' I replied. 'He's a politician, but he's into all kinds of dodgy shit. He's got fucken heaps of money, so there's no problem there. You know, the bloke can fix things.'

Shit, where did that come from? A corrupt politician as a relative? That was the first and last time I used that story, but it seemed to do the trick. Patty liked the sound of a Mr Fix-it in his corner.

'Can he stop the coppers?'

'He won't have to stop them. He'd know before it started.'

A satisfied Patty returned to dealing mode again. 'So, how much do ya reckon you'll want, then?'

'Not sure yet but, you know, fifty pounds sounds about right,' I replied. I was taking a huge risk. I knew that it was a bloody big leap in quantity from an ounce to fifty pounds, but I felt more comfortable planting the seed with Patty. Let him do all the work convincing Medici that I could be trusted. Now that I had political muscle in my corner, I was sure that Patty was onside.

'No worries. I'll give you the exact prices when you call me.'

'Rightio.'

I pulled up in front of Patty's house after he gave me last-minute directions. 'Hold on a sec. Take this, mate,' I said, reaching into my jeans and pulling out two hundreds.

'Thanks, mate. See ya.'

Head down, Patty walked up his driveway. He had become hired help, a dog waiting for scraps.

Four

June 6-17, 1992

Every operative does things differently, but I believe that controlling a target from day one is the cornerstone of effective undercover work. If you're firm from the first meeting, it makes it easier to manipulate them when buy/bust day comes along. Once that foundation's in place, compromises are almost out of the question because the target has been 'trained' to act in a certain way.

After the second drug buy I felt like I had total control over Patty Condro, but the main man was another matter. Medici had a history of unpredictable behaviour, of being the type of bloke you couldn't push around. His father found this out the hard way. Still, control is one thing, and greed is another. Money can be a great little motivator.

I spent the next couple of days transcribing tapes from the wires. After a few hours of listening to Patty Condro's party trick of a voice I needed a break, so I popped in on Special Projects Unit (SPU) for an update on Medici's telephone intercepts.

SPU (pronounced 'spew') was in the St Kilda Road complex, about five minutes from Russell Street. Their job was to monitor telephone intercepts. Now and again, one or two of the uniformed coppers from SPU tended to take their job a little too seriously. I remember on one operation a target was using 'chocolates' as a code for heroin.

Damian Marrett

'Mate, I've got the chocolates,' he said to me over the phone.

'Chocolates? What fucken chocolates?'

'You know...'

'No, what chocolates?'

'The, er, heroin,' he said in a whisper. Like lowering your voice wouldn't be picked up by an intercept.

'Ah, the heroin.'

'Yeah.'

'Okay, I get it. From now on it's chocolates.'

Personally, I thought it was a part of my job as an undercover to make him translate the code. I already knew the crim was stupid, so I really had nothing to fear. Still, my phone rang five minutes later. It was one of the SPU boys giving me some professional advice: 'Damian, you must respect the codes. The crooks become suspicious if you don't.'

'Relax, mate,' I said to him. 'I've done it for a reason.'

Months later in court, whenever chocolates were mentioned on a telephone intercept, it had already been established that we were really talking about heroin. It saved me a lot of time in the witness box.

Anyway, Medici's phone had already been bugged thanks to the aborted Operation Reuben, and a few pages related to Bert or me directly had been set aside by SPU.

'I wouldn't fuck with him, mate,' Patty said at one point. 'I know he's only a kid, but there's something about him, something about his eyes.'

'You reckon he's fair dinkum? He'll come up with the money?' Medici asked.

'Mate, I know him. He might look like a kid, but he can do it,' replied Patty. 'Don't make the mistake of fucking him around because he looks like a kid.'

'All right, I'll start organising, but you better not be wrong, Patty.'

'And he's got crazy eyes,' Patty added inexplicably.

When I returned to Russell Street and outlined the conversation to Googa, we laughed at the absurdity of it all. And from that moment on, I had a nickname, a lasting legacy of Operation Bert — 'The Kid' (not 'Crazy Eyes'). Even now people still call me 'kid', and we're talking over ten years later.

At any rate, it appeared that Patty had fallen head over heels into line behind me. He was delivering all our messages, and vouching for us behind the scenes. Medici probably needed a little more convincing, but I knew that the lure of filthy lucre would prove to be his prime motivation.

It wasn't until Saturday June 13, two days later, that I phoned Patty.

'G'day Patty, it's Damian.' I was tempted to call myself 'The Crazy-eyed Kid', but resisted the urge.

'Hi, mate. How's things?'

'Well, not great, to tell you the truth. That sample was shit,' I said. The ounce of speed had already been spot tested in our forensics lab. It came back at 7.1 per cent amphetamine sulphate and 72.8 per cent ephedrine (the net effective strength of this combination would produce an effect similar to 15 per cent pure amphetamine. Pretty poor sales pitch from Medici).

'Ah, fuck, fuck.'

'Tell Vince to ring me, Patty, or it's off. That thing was bullshit.'

'Fuck, yeah, okay. I'll get Vince to call ya.'

An hour later, Medici was on the hello phone. I saw this an ideal opportunity to get on the front foot.

'G'day Damian, it's Ma ... Vince here.' Stupid dickhead nearly called himself Matt. 'Mate, off the bat, I've gotta apologise to ya. I got fucked around because I got it off a different bloke.'

'So how do I know we'll be right from now on?'

''Cause this time it'll come from the place it's made, you know what I mean?' Medici was alluding to the fact that the next batch would come to us directly from the source, the laboratory.

'There'll be a fucken heap of cash involved, Vince. I've gotta know that you can do this thing. It's a bit of a worry when the first one's not up to scratch.'

'Mate, all I can say is I'm sorry,' Medici said. 'It won't happen again. It's coming from the place.'

'I'm gonna have to test it before I give you the money,' I said, knowing full well it was a hollow threat. We'd bust him before his goods had a chance to go under the microscope. 'That thing you gave me was shit.'

'Yeah, yeah, I fucken know,' he said, beginning to get frustrated. 'Mate, trust me, it'll be fine. How much will you be wanting anyway?'

'My man wants as much as you can get your hands on. How's fifty sound for starters?'

'Um, yeah, should be right. Leave it with me, okay?'

'All right, you sort things out your end, and I'll talk to you soon. Also I wanna firm up those prices.'

'I'll get onto Patty, and he'll work it out with ya.'

The next day, I spoke to Patty. I was in the perfect bargaining position after what had transpired the day before. We agreed upon seventeen grand a pound for the amphetamines, and $4300 a pound of cannabis. I also laid down some ground rules for the transaction:

Undercover

1. It's my call on the whereabouts of the location.
2. Any transaction must be conducted out in the open.
3. I want to see the gear before I give away the money.
4. No guns.

I also said that I was keen to do the deal early next week.

This operation was quickly becoming a large one. If all went to plan, I'd be rocking up with more than a million dollars in cash for the drugs — $1 065 000 of taxpayers' money, to be precise — to this day, still a record amount of Victoria Police 'show' money for the one buy/bust.

I knew that the police budget would be stretched, and on the Monday morning it played out that way. Word had filtered down that the deal was creating a few headaches with the bean-counters.

For a start, the Treasury Department wouldn't release amounts of money that exceeded a million. Major problem. But, for the moment, their problem, not mine. I'd worry about all that sort of shit only if I had to.

Monday afternoon I rang Patty to confirm the deal was going ahead, but no answer. This was no good. Once again, my thoughts turned to the scope of the deal. Had he and Medici gone cold on the whole arrangement?

I wandered down to SPU for an update on Medici's movements. He'd been on the road, travelling to Adelaide. This information had been confirmed by the Australian Federal Police (AFP) in South Australia (Drug Squad members had been liaising with the AFP since the commencement of Operation Reuben). It appeared that Medici's amphetamine suppliers were Adelaide-based. As a result, it also appeared that the operation was still on track.

Damian Marrett

I arrived back at the office an hour later, and my anxieties vanished when Patty called. The deal was set for Wednesday morning. We were definitely on.

From that point, the Drug Squad was buzzing. Hire cars and accommodation were lined up, the dogs (surveillance) and the soggies (Special Operations Group) were kept up to speed, bust and distress signals were chosen, listening devices were checked and rechecked, and radios were decoded to ensure they were all on the same frequency for the big day.

Still, there was that little matter with the Treasury budget. Would they cough up the $1.065 mill? Tuesday morning we had ourselves an answer when the cash was picked up, no questions asked. The job was on.

That afternoon, about 100 of us cleared to the Sportslander Hotel in Echuca, about an hour's drive east of Swan Hill. We hired out the whole hotel, but no suspicions were raised. June's a quiet month, and the owners were just happy to flash up the 'No Vacancy' sign. They didn't even ask what we were up to. Probably didn't want to know.

After everyone arrived, we conducted a mass briefing outside. Two hours later everyone was geared up and ready to go, so we cracked open a few cans. At 3 a.m. I was in fellow undercover Kim Culpin's room, drinking, flirting, talking shit. Googa cracked it, paying us a late-night visit in his singlet and boxer jocks. Even when Googa looked like Homer Simpson, you did what he said. Bedtime, Damian.

Wednesday morning, and a six-thirty briefing. Detective Sergeant Chris Murphy was my controller for the buy/bust. An ex-undercover who was in the know, Murph had spent a year undercover in Mildura back in the eighties. He knew how these people operated.

It was outlined how the job was to run. Distress and bust signals were confirmed, radios were tested, and our vehicle had already been fitted with a covert video-recording device planted in the centre console. My specific instructions were to secure a location site, and ensure Medici was given no money until both the cannabis and the amphetamines were in our possession.

At nine-thirty Lordy and I raced around to pick up Patty at his home in Tresco. I was driving a Nissan Pajero, an empty greyhound trailer latched onto the back of it. The trailer had been hired for the storing and transportation of the drugs once the deal was completed. After a few toots of the horn, Patty eventually waddled his way into the back seat.

'Everything the same?' I asked.

'Yep. He rang me fifteen minutes ago,' replied Patty.

'So he's got all the gear, has he?'

'As far as I know, everything's hunky-dory.'

'Right, we're off then,' I said, pointing the car towards Mildura.

Two hours later we pulled up beside the Sturt Highway on the northeastern outskirts of Mildura. Medici's silver Fairlane was waiting for us on the side of the road. As I turned off the engine, Medici, dressed in his signature silver suit, jumped in the back seat with Patty. Neville Wise was also tagging along.

'G'day Vince. How ya going?' asked Lordy.

'Good. G'day Damian.'

'How are ya?'

'All right. Everything's sweet on both counts. We'll pick the green up here, right?'

'What?'

'You'll get the green here,' Medici said. He looked over at me. I did not look happy. 'Ah, you don't want to take it now?'

'We want to take it all together,' I replied.

'No, we've got a bit of a drive to get the white. This is what he told me. We've got to pick it up this time. Next time they'll come even as far as your place, you know.'

This was exactly the sort of situation we had feared. I was in for a battle. On reflection, I'd probably gone a bit overboard on volume; in my exuberance to nail these blokes I should've started the bidding a little lower. Even five pounds of amphetamines would scare off a lot of would-be dealers so early on in a relationship. If that was the case, fifty pounds was somewhat stretching their resources and trust.

'Well, how far off is the white?' I asked.

'We're about, it's, um, in South Australia, mate,' Medici said.

'How quick can you get it over here?'

'The next one they'll bring as far as your joint,' he said. 'Look, I'm going to be quite frank with you, right. He's never met anyone who'll take fifty pounds at a time. He told me straight out that he thinks it's a set-up. I said, "Mate, don't even fucken think of telling me things like that, because we haven't got a deal from now on if you keep going like that." He goes, "Look, I wanna make sure on the first one." But, you know, he's all ready.'

'What are the arrangements to get the white then?' I asked.

'They're waiting for us. They were expecting us this morning.'

'In South Aussie?'

'Yeah, this afternoon. I told him not this morning 'cause my bloke hasn't turned up yet. He said to me, "You're not fucking me around." I said, "No, no, this guy wouldn't fuck us around. They're serious."'

'Well, we're not going to South Aussie,' I said.

'Aren't ya?'

'That was the deal from the start. You said you'd get fifty of each for us here, and we've got it' — the cash — 'floating around here.'

We were looking at a stalemate. From our end, the deals (meaning, our money) couldn't be separated, so I bunkered down for a shit-fight. Medici then told me that his suppliers only wanted to do a five-pound deal anyway.

'He told me straight out that he's never met anyone buying that big, you know.'

'We've bought that big fucken heaps,' I lied.

'Mate, I'm not doubting your word.'

'I doubt if coppers would buy that big, to tell you the truth,' I lied, not for the first time.

'Like I said, I'm with ya, mate. I've had a fucken ... I've been up to Patty's place, right, I've been to Adelaide the other day. We had problems with the guy because he didn't want to do it after I'd lined it up with you. I promised you something, and he didn't want to come to the party. I told Patty to put him in the car, and we took him down to the river, and I said, "Right, it's either fifty or I'll do ya right now. Simple as that. I don't give a fuck who ya work for or who ya don't work for, I don't give a fuck. I'll waste ya. Simple as that." I said, "I'm not gonna look stupid in front of my people. First of all, they're gonna tell me I'm a bullshit artist." You know, I don't bullshit about things like that. I was gonna waste him there and then. He was fucken OD'ing mate, 'cause he thought — not thought — he *knew* his life was in fucken danger.'

O-*kay*. That whole pathetic Medici monologue was done for my benefit, trying to convince me that he'd done his best. To be honest, it wasn't very convincing. Sure, he'd had arguments with his supplier over the details, but I suspected he would've been a little more civil than issuing multiple death threats.

'We told our boss that you were right, you know, don't worry,' said Lordy. 'We've met them twice, you know, it's not a problem. We bloody stuck our neck out. Why can't he do us a favour?'

'Yeah,' said Patty, sensing a moment to test out his voice.

'See, we have like, it's like a little fucken company, our thing. We have rules, you know, policies,' I added, relating the way our fictitious drug-dealing operation ran its business affairs. But I could've been talking about Victoria Police Drug Squad procedures just as easily.

'I understand,' said Medici, not really understanding the predicament I was in.

We then decided that we needed to take a breather. Medici would ring his supplier to see if anything could be arranged without us having to leave Victoria, while Lordy and I cruised around town in search of a bite to eat. I rang Murph. He said to hang in there, and also to let them know that we were in no rush — the deal could be done tomorrow.

Half an hour later we drove to the Target car park in Mildura to meet Medici and Patty once again. Both of them jumped into the back seat.

'Well, we just rang our man,' I said. 'He said that it's here or nothing, but he's given us another day. I said to him, "How about if I just travel a couple of hundred more Ks?" And he said, "Get back in the car and fucken come back if you're gonna start that shit."'

Medici didn't like the sound of that, but he was prepared to state his case for the defence anyway. 'He guarantees you a free fucken run all the way from Adelaide to Mildura. No worries, he reckons.'

'You see, Victoria I'm not worried about, all right, Vince. But South Aussie, not a chance.'

I left it in their heads to work out why we couldn't leave the state, but I was pretty sure that Patty would've relayed the 'politician as an uncle' story. There was no need for me to join the dots for them.

Medici then made a call to his South Australian supplier on his mobile. Five minutes later, finally, a compromise, and also a transparent play for more money upfront.

'Okay, I've just been speaking to Chocko in Adelaide. Patty and I are prepared to drive over there to pick up the gear, but we need fifty grand from you blokes.'

'Nah, nah, no way. The money doesn't get divvied up. I can show you the money now if you want, but it's going nowhere until we see the gear.'

Medici collected himself. He figured that I had the money, but he also knew that I wasn't going to separate it. 'All right, all right, we'll do this thing then. Next time he'll drive it to Melbourne for ya, but we'll sort it out this time.'

'Well, next time we'll know that, you know. We rocked up today thinking it was all ready to go,' I said.

'Yeah, I know. Look, while we're gone, both you guys are welcome at my house if you like, to relax a little bit.'

'No, we should be right,' I said, incapable of imagining Lordy and I kicking back in front of Medici's telly watching *A Current Affair*.

'We haven't caught up with Graham yet,' chimed in Lordy. 'He's the poor prick driving around with it' — the one million in cash — 'you know.'

'Yeah, we'd better fill him in,' I said.

'And we can also go to a chemist that can sell me some fucken drugs,' said Lordy, suffering from a bout of the flu.

'Chemist?' Medici replied, his wires completely crossed. 'Don't go asking for anything around here. Don't go for hits, mate.'

'No, I mean for me cold,' Lordy answered.

Medici wasn't listening. He was certain that Lordy was looking to buy some smack in his patch. 'I wouldn't do it. They'll get the jacks onto you straightaway.'

I interrupted the confusion for everyone's benefit. 'Rightio then, we'll hear from you. We're all sort of stuck now.'

'Don't worry, mate. It'll work out. We're crooks, but we're good crooks.'

'Nice crooks,' I said as a joke.

'Nah, we're good crooks.' The humour was lost on Medici. He was too busy trying to sound genuine. As always he came up short, sounding more like a tosser instead.

'Thanks for that, mate. I'll ring you in the morning.'

'No worries. Oh yeah, I've got that coke for you too,' he said.

At our second meeting I'd briefly discussed the possibility of buying cocaine off Medici in the future. He'd remembered. 'How much?'

'That's three. How's five hundred sound?'

'Fine, but I've got no money on me.'

'No worries,' Medici said, palming me a three-gram sample. 'Fix us up tomorrow.'

'Yeah, I'll do that.'

Medici and Condro then hopped out of our vehicle, and left the car park in the silver Fairlane. A ten-hour round trip ahead of them, it was quite the magnanimous gesture.

As we drove away, I spoke clearly into the recording device.

'The time is 1:15 p.m. It's Wednesday the 17th of June, 1992. This is Detective Senior Constable Damian Marrett attached to the Drug Squad. With me is Detective Senior Constable Lord. We're currently leaving the Target car park in Mildura after a discussion with targets Matt Medici and Patty Condro. Both targets will now be travelling to Adelaide to pick up fifty pounds of amphetamines. I'll be calling target Medici tomorrow to discuss the situation further, and to organise the details of the proposed buy/bust. I'll stop the device here at about 1:16 p.m.'

Five

June 18, 1992

The next morning, it was another early start. After a quick briefing I rang Medici at his home before 8 a.m. He'd just swung through the door after pulling an all-nighter with Patty. The amphetamines had been collected from Adelaide, but he was only able to get his hands on thirty-five pounds of marijuana for the second part of the deal. I wasn't particularly concerned. Besides the fact that the speed was the main sticking point, jail time for trafficking amphetamines was significantly higher than a cannabis charge.

Thirty minutes later, Lordy and I met with two very tired boys at the Apex Caravan Park in Mildura.

'Mate, I've got little eyes. I've been on the fucken road. No sleep,' said Medici, trailing off.

'Mate, I'm appreciative,' I said. 'We had a fucken prick of a time too. Our man wanted us to leave last night. Just take the money and come home. Had to bloody talk him round.'

'Well, how do you want to do this, then?' asked Medici.

'You've got a tow ball on your car?'

'Yeah,' said Medici.

'Just take our trailer and load it up,' I said. 'We'll wait here for you. When you come back, we'll switch the trailer over.'

'Call in our money man, and the job's done,' added Lordy.

'I've been sitting here for about an hour and I've watched. I mean, I reckon this place is perfect,' I followed up.

And it *was* perfect: the dogs and the soggies had checked out this location thoroughly. Our snipers were in perfect positions — poised and ready to shoot — surveillance cameras were pointed our way, there were plenty of hiding spots for cover, and any traffic in or out could easily be monitored.

Medici was less enthusiastic about the suitability. 'Mate, I know this area well. I don't live far from here, and it's fucken dangerous, I can tell you that now. There's people down here who stick their nose in where it doesn't belong.'

'It's not going to look suss if we just take this off, put it on yours, and it's like you're just picking up a trailer,' said Lordy, pointing at our dog transporter.

'I'd like to show you the spot that I've picked out for us,' said a disinterested Medici. 'My bloke also wants to have a look at the cash. He's already here. It took us ages to get the stuff in the bloody panels, and he won't hand over the car until he sees the money.'

'You can't take any away though,' I said.

'No, no. He just wants to look, Damian, then it's all set,' chipped in Patty. 'I'm just in the midst of it all. I'm fucked. I don't know what's fucken going on. I've been sitting in the back of a car since yesterday, that's all I know.'

'Bloody I've been up all night too,' said a flu-ridden Lordy. 'I'm just surprised I've got any lungs left.'

At this moment, Vincenzo 'Jim' Ventrice got out of Medici's car. A slim, long-haired bloke in his mid-twenties, neatly dressed in jeans and buttoned-up pink shirt, he looked a bit more placid than Medici, and a lot more refined than Patty, his toy poodle mullet hairstyle not withstanding.

After handshakes and introductions Ventrice immediately proceeded to try to steer the conversation back on track. It was hard work when everyone couldn't keep their eyes open or had come down with a nasty bug.

'All I want is when it gets here, we do it my way, that's all,' Ventrice said quietly but firmly. 'You come with me now, with the money. You give me the money, and I'll give you the car.'

'We're not moving from here because our bloke already knows we're here. If we ring him and tell him that we're moving again, he'll send our money back because of all the fuck-ups yesterday,' I said.

'Mate, I'm fucken freaking out too. I've lost a fucken lot of sleep, a lot of fucken time,' said Medici. I could tell he was about to lose it again.

'That's why we won't fuck around today,' I said, trying to head him off.

Too late. He was off.

'I want it to fucken finish. Otherwise I'm going to fucken start to get fucked off because I've done all this driving. All night, last night, I stayed awake. We only just got back home, right, so I've put my fucken arse on the line, right. We went and done all this, all this thing, you know, and we done it in favour to both parties, right, because we want it to happen.'

'Look, we don't want to be rooting around either. We want to just get it over and done with, and head back,' I said truthfully.

'Well, it's going to take probably five hours to get here anyway,' said Ventrice.

'Another five hours? That's bullshit. What was the bloody overnight drive for then?' I asked.

'Mate, that's the quickest I can do it,' said Ventrice, ignoring the question. 'I need to know the money's here.'

'I fucken said to Vince yesterday, "Do ya wanna see the cash?" I fucken could've shown it to him then.'

'But I haven't seen it,' Ventrice said firmly.

'Surely you could've taken his word.'

'Not really. Not when I've gotta send that much over, you know what I mean. It's a little bit different. As soon as I see the money I'll make a phone call, and it's on its way.'

This was really starting to piss me off. I had no idea what game they were playing at now. Medici and Patty apparently drove overnight to get the gear, but then apparently didn't pick it up. For all we knew, though, the speed could've been close by.

'Mate, I don't like it here,' said Medici, unable to focus on anything but the suitability of the transaction site. 'We're gonna cop a couple of fucken bricks for it, a couple of bricks. Ten years is a fucken brick, right.'

'Well, if it's going to be five hours, what I'll do is, I'll find a more secluded place, right,' I said, trying to take control again.

Medici interrupted. 'I've got two places in mind. Just come by yourselves and check it out. You and I can go. Patty and you can stay here,' he said, referring to Lordy.

'I told Patty right from the start that when we do the thing, it's my location,' I said. 'I didn't argue about price, so don't argue with this one.'

'Too dangerous, mate.'

I was adamant. 'I'll find another one. It'll take me an hour.'

Medici couldn't be stuffed arguing any more. 'All right.'

A victory at last, I then rang for the money. One of the SOG boys, Spocky, had the loot in the boot of a white Ford Laser. After making the call, I rejoined the group. They were a miserable lot.

'I just want to go home and go to bed,' said poor old Patty.

'Have you been up all night too?' Lordy asked Medici. My partner was clearly delirious with flu.

'Been up all night, all right ...' replied Medici.

'Well, next time I'll stay up all night,' I said, throwing in my $0.02 worth. The whole conversation was getting just a bit tiresome for my liking, crap pun intended.

'You wouldn't think you've been up all night. You look a million dollars, as usual,' said Lordy to his new best mate, Medici.

'Yeah, but I don't fucken feel it,' Medici said, wearing the same silver suit he had on the day before. You could tell that he was just itching to throw on a different set of threads.

'Jesus you're a suck,' I said to Lordy, acting out a bit of a good crook/bad crook scenario. We both knew that Medici needed his ego stroked, and Lordy was prepared to do that. I couldn't do it, because the minute I did, Medici would be on the front foot again with everything going his way. My role was to remind him that I was encountering problems behind the scenes, too.

The Laser with the cash in the boot entered the car park, and Ventrice followed me over to the rear of the car. Spocky popped the hatch, and I opened the lid of a large green toolbox. I removed some loose tools, and then Jim flicked through the notes underneath — $1 065 000, all in $10 000 bundles of hundred dollar notes, give or take five grand. Although Ventrice didn't count every single note, he appeared satisfied.

Spocky took off, and we returned to the group. 'Okay, I'll make the phone call, and we're on,' said Ventrice.

'We're going to find another place then,' I said, now

Undercover

wary of the fact that I didn't want to cop a couple of those bricks Medici was banging on about. 'We won't tell the boss in Melbourne though. I'm just, you know, if something goes wrong now, I really am fucked. But you blokes are happy, right?'

'Yeah, that's all right, yeah,' said Ventrice.

'We've got the phone on,' Lordy said. 'We'll just stay in the centre of town, because when we get out of town the signal goes.'

At 8:50 a.m. the three of them left in Medici's Fairlane. A short time later I met up with Murph and explained the situation to him. Because we were using a recording and not a listening device he was unaware of what had just transpired. But even if he had heard it all, we would've met up anyway. Details sometimes get confused when you're in the thick of it.

Murph suggested our second-choice location could be used for the buy/bust — the Mildura Ski Club (water not snow). He also told us to keep pushing for the deals to be done concurrently.

After a phone call from Medici at about 11:30 a.m. I met up with the three dealers in the Target car park. We then went inside the shopping centre for coffee and cake. On the walk to the café, I became aware that two others in the vicinity were monitoring the situation, and they were not batting for our team. Probably Ventrice's Adelaide mates looking out for him.

Sometimes I could sense that others were watching me, especially when I was carrying large amounts of cash — yet on this occasion I wasn't. I guess it's the same for anyone. If you'd just withdrawn ten grand in cash from the bank, you'd be a lot more conscious of who was between you and your car.

Damian Marrett

The reasons why people kept watch on me varied. It could be as simple as some bloke providing lookout in a car. Other times someone could be waiting for the signal to supply me with drugs. If ever there was half a chance, I'd nick off from the crooks and pass on the information to my controller by phone. Then we could keep an eye on them keeping an eye on us, but there was no such chance today.

Having said all that, Ventrice's pals (if they were connected to him) weren't being obvious about their intentions, but they didn't belong in a shopping centre at midday. Pensioners and prams did. Italians with dark glasses didn't.

When we were seated at the café, Ventrice handed me a blue Shoei motorcycle helmet bag. He wanted me to place $300 000 into it, presumably his cut of the deal. Who knew how the rest of the $550 000 for the white would be divvied up? But it did explain one thing: there was a very good reason why Medici was so eager to keep the deal on track. No doubt he'd end up with the bulk of the cash. Even Patty's cut would be worth a sleepless night.

After the meeting, I had a couple of hours to spare while the crooks got their shit together. I checked in with Murph; he told me that the operation had to be concluded today or it would be aborted. The show money — the $1 065 000 we showed Ventrice and Medici — was needed to pay meal allowance claims and police overtime. Budgets were that tight, and this only added to the frustration. On any undercover job, you'd much prefer to let some of the money run in order to maintain credibility with the target(s). Mind you, one million bucks — or even the cannabis component of $200 000 — was probably way too much money to let run. I doubted we'd see the cash again when the second deal was due to take place.

Undercover

I also received a prescient and timely warning from the SOG boys. 'Dame, if things turn shitty, don't freak out if you see a little red light on one of the targets,' said one of the ninjas. 'It's just an infrared tracker from one of the snipers' guns over the other side of the river. You'll only see it for a second. He'll be dead the next.' Comforting.

At 2:45 p.m. Lordy and I were waiting in a car park near the Mildura Ski Club. Five minutes later our targets pulled up in the Fairlane. Unfortunately, the news was no better.

'They still want us to do the green first,' said Medici.

'This is bullshit. We'll do the fucken green if you show us the powders,' I fired back. I had to take the initiative. This was going nowhere.

'I've fucken told those cunts in Adelaide. They're fucken scared of me, so don't you fucken push me,' said a fuming Medici. 'You know, I've felt like this before and you don't wanna fucken know.'

Shit ... Time to reel him in. 'Mate, we're not being unreasonable here. We've been fair with you blokes all along, you know that.'

Medici calmed himself momentarily. 'Yeah, you know we want it just as much as you blokes want it. I just, fucken, I'm getting to the stage where I'm starting to get fucken spin-outs.'

'You're not on your own there,' said Lordy. 'What sort of business is he running? He won't even let us take a look at the gear.'

Instead of punching something or someone, Medici paced over to the side of us in order to make yet another phone call.

With his boss out of earshot, Patty seized the moment. 'Oh mate, I'm going bananas, ya know. I mean, I feel like hopping in the car and going back home. I'm sick of the whole fucken thing. I mean, it's not as if I'm getting anything out of it unless you blokes … ya know what I mean.'

Patty was after more money, but I let that double-cut request fly through to the keeper. 'They're doing themselves out of business,' I said, "cause we're not going to deal with them again if they don't show us. I mean, do they know that?'

'I've told them that, I've told them that, I've told them that,' replied Patty on repeat. 'I've been battling black and blue. All I want to do is go home and go to fucken sleep. I'm sick of the whole fucken charade.'

Patty's voice was wavering, and when Medici rejoined us he was a broken man too. 'They're still fucken solid. We've been busting our balls for fucken two days and nights. I might as well get a taxi sign and slap it on top of me fucken car. We haven't had anything to eat in fucken two days and two nights, mate. I'm starting to see dark shadows.'

Dark shadows? I couldn't help thinking of the scores of surveillance crew less than a hundred metres away from us. But those dark shadows were a product of his weary mind, not dogs behind trees.

'I've got other people in Melbourne that we can do business with,' said an uncharacteristically riled Patty. The cup of coffee must have kicked in. 'It's their fucken loss, my fucken gain, and they can go and get fucked. If they want to change their mind, they change their mind.'

'Tell them if they want to do business, come back here at four o'clock,' I said. 'Otherwise, forget it. If he's got any other queries, Patty, just put him on the phone, and I'll fucken have a go at him.'

'Put it this way, um, that's what I'm going to tell him now.'

Undercover

And, with that, a delirious Patty was on the move, all fired up to fulfil his chief negotiating role with the Adelaide speed suppliers. Medici went along for the ride.

I wasn't confident. No one was. Time was running out, and we were no nearer to a solution than we had been early yesterday morning. It was understandable. Splitting the deals was their insurance if the whole thing turned to shit. In our corner, we couldn't let money run. Our options were limited.

Meeting with Murph, we were told to do the cannabis deal separately if we had to, but make a huge play to get the speed to the location. At the same time I was strapped with a listening device to sit alongside the recording one. One way or another, we were closing in on a bust.

One hour later, Medici called with an apology. It was green followed by white. The speed deal was in a perilous position.

'Tell them to fuck off then,' I said. 'Bring the green and we're out of here. They can fuck right off.' I didn't really mean what I was saying, but I was trying a last-ditch attempt to force their hand. We were just hoping they were bluffing, and that both deals would be done simultaneously at the last minute.

It was bad news but, in reality, the delivery of the speed was just the icing on the cake. Everyone would be slapped with a conspiracy to traffic charge anyway. There was nothing else we could do but accept the offer.

Medici did relay some good news though. He was now able to sell us forty-three pounds. They must've been able to scrounge another eight pounds in the meantime.

Ten minutes later, our targets were back at the ski club ready to do a grass deal.

'Mate, we apologise for all this shit. We just rang up Melbourne to try and set up fifty for you there. Should have something for you Saturday arvo,' said Medici, still clinging by his fingernails to the deal. 'And that fucken five hundred, don't worry about it. It's sweet.'

'Rightio,' I said, twigging that he was referring to the earlier cocaine deal.

'I've only got one problem before we do it,' Patty said. 'None of youse have got a piece on ya?'

Lordy and I looked at each other, both saying no.

''Cause none of us have. I've made sure on my end, you know what I mean?' No, I didn't really know what he meant. We weren't carrying a gun, but I had a feeling that Medici might be. Probably asked Patty to make sure that he was the only one.

Medici then showed me the rear of his hand. On it, he had scrawled $184 900 in blue ink — the amount of money we owed him for the forty-three pounds of cannabis. 'That sound right to you?' he asked.

'What's this bit down here?' I asked, pointing to a smudge underneath the amount.

'That was the $500 for the coke, but I was just saying to Patty coming here, fuck it.'

'What is it, then?' I asked, one time for the tape.

'One eight four, nine hundred.'

Medici then made a call on his phone, and a minute later a green Ford sedan entered the car park. Neville Wise was behind the wheel.

'Who's this bloke then?' asked Lordy.

'Neville,' replied Patty. 'You know Neville.'

'Yeah, oh yeah.'

'You've already met him, you know, that way you know who you're dealing with.'

I moved over to the Ford and clicked open the boot. In the back of my mind I was still quietly hopeful that a

Undercover

second car would appear around the corner with a boot full of amphetamines. You never know — they might take the bait and get greedy at the last minute.

The boot was chockers. Two large suitcases contained fifteen pounds each of cannabis wrapped in plastic bags. Another five large garbage bags were also stashed full of dope. It looked like it was all there. Time for the bust signal.

'I reckon Googa will be happy with this, then,' I said to Lordy.

'Yeah, no worries,' he agreed.

'As long as Googa's happy, you know. He's the only bloke I've gotta please.' No harm in throwing in another signal if the bust team missed the word Googa the first time.

'Mate, we're still trying. We haven't given up yet,' said Medici, still trying to push the possibility of a Melbourne speed deal.

'Better get onto Graham and give him a call, then we can head back,' said Lordy, trying to open the lock on the dog trailer. Graham was Spocky, our money-man in the white Laser.

'Yeah, I'll give him a call now,' I said, well aware that the soggies were yet to make an appearance. Maybe the bust signal hadn't been heard.

I rang the Operations Commander to call in the money. Or in other words, 'Come on, fellas, bust time.'

The phone answered on the first ring. 'Yeah, bring in the money, mate.'

'What? What do you mean?' He was in another world.

'Yep, bring it in mate. The green's all here. Googa'll be happy.'

'So, now you want the money?'

'Yeah, we're ready to go, mate.'

Silence, and then he cottoned on. 'Bust! Bust! Bust!'

I hung up the phone and walked back to the trailer. The boys were trustful enough to let us pack the grass before the money was due to arrive, but Lordy was still fiddling with the trailer's lock.

'Graham's on his way.'

'No problems. We trust you blokes. Youse have done everything right so far. Just whack it in there,' said Patty, the trailer's doors now both open.

'You reckon Googa will be happy with it?' I asked Lordy, not for the first bloody time.

'Well, we'll just have to tell him that we bent over backwards to help these blokes with the white, but they just couldn't help us,' said Lordy, turfing bags of grass from the boot into the trailer.

Half a minute passed. I was starting to freak out, and was thinking about making another call. Seconds later a van cruised slowly through the car park. The SOGs' van. No one even gave it a second glance.

As soon as the van passed us it suddenly pulled up, and a team of a dozen soggies dressed like paramilitary ninjas spewed out of the back. They were fully wound up. 'Police! Don't move! Hands in the air! Get on the fucken ground, don't fucken move!'

And then a gunshot went off. From where, I had no idea.

Instinctively I hit the deck, tossing the mobile phone in the air. I looked behind me. Medici was running towards the water, flinging a pistol in an arc. Lying prick had a gun the whole time. The weapon hit the water with a thwack. If I hadn't seen it, video surveillance would've picked it up, their camera aimed squarely at the action from the other bank of the Murray.

Undercover

After the initial confusion, I stretched myself out on the ground and didn't move a hair. Neither did anyone else. I just lay there with a soggie's boot dug forcefully into my back.

Five minutes later I was handcuffed and arrested with the lot of them, standard procedure in a buy/bust. It makes good sense to scoop up everyone at the end of an operation, rather than declare our hand. As a result, the crooks don't know what's going on. It's just like keeping an ace up your sleeve. Later, you might be put into the cells with the targets to glean further information. Also, some crooks employed back-up at purchase sites. If I jumped up and started slapping backs and shaking hands with the boys in blue, who knows what could have happened?

A few minutes later, we were put in different cars. It was only then that I could relax.

'Well done, Dame,' said Phil Strawhorn. 'Bloody good work.'

'Jesus, who fired that shot?' I asked.

'One of the soggies tripped when he came out of the van. His finger was on the trigger,' he laughed.

'Fucken hell. Scared the shit out of me.'

'Scared the shit out of you? What about poor Patty Condro? He actually did shit himself. Don't think it was the gunshot though.'

Jesus. 'Lying bastards,' I smiled. 'They told me they hadn't eaten for a couple of days.'

While we were being driven to the Mildura police station our crew was raiding houses, and rounding up the rest of Medici's mob. Ventrice was nabbed only a short distance away from the ski club. He didn't have the fifty pounds of amphetamines on him. Our intelligence told us that the speed was in Mildura the whole time, but finding it was another matter.

Back at the station word had got around that Matt Medici, the local kingpin, had been arrested. The local coppers couldn't contain their joy.

I ended up in an interview room with Detective Sergeant Steve 'Coach' Cody, handcuffed to keep up the charade. Coach could tell the cuffs were giving me grief so he slipped out to look for the keys, leaving the door ajar.

I kept myself amused by playing Harry Houdini. Just as I had my arms tucked underneath my thighs, two young local coppers popped their heads in. One was in uniform, the other in plain clothes. I sat up straight, immediately feeling vulnerable.

'What are *you* fucken looking at, ya drug-dealing piece of shit?' the one in plain clothes said.

I looked away, not a word. But I couldn't think of anything worse than copping a beating in handcuffs. I understood their reaction, though. Anybody connected to Medici in Mildura would not get an easy ride. He was a hated man.

'Smartarse prick,' the uniformed one said, walking towards me.

Just as both of them were about to give me a hard time, Coach rescued me with the keys. 'I'll take care of him, fellas,' he said. They walked out with a swagger.

In the next interview room, the last word went to Patty Condro. A dumb-fuck to the end. After his arrest, he was questioned by two in my crew.

'This is Senior Detective Phil Strawhorn of the Victoria Police Drug Squad. Also present is Senior Detective Tom Ridley. I'm taping an interview with Patty Condro. Patty Condro, I intend to interview you in relation to trafficking in drugs of dependence. Do you agree that the time is now 7:10 p.m.?' Phil then directed Patty to the analogue clock hanging on the wall to the side of him.

Patty squinted at it, before saying, 'Um, I don't know. I can't tell the time on one of them clocks.'

Postscript

The car full of amphetamines that we suspected was in the Mildura area was never recovered.

Medici's 9 mm automatic pistol, fished out of the Murray River, had been originally stolen from a South Australian policewoman.

Come the committal hearing, Medici's defence team trotted out the old 'IQ of 76' line again. They argued that Medici lived a Walter Mitty–type existence — the drug transactions were all a flight of fancy, a sham concocted by a mental retard. According to his solicitors, Medici was in way over his head.

Ventrice's lawyer said my version of events were 'a litany of nonsense'. Patty Condro's counsel described his client as a minor player in proceedings, dubbing him Patty the Patsy.

When I was questioned in court about the validity of this claim, I responded that Patty 'had his moments of stardom'.

GOING DOWN

List of Principal Charges and Sentences

Matteo Rosario MEDICI
- 7 charges of trafficking a drug of dependence
- 5 charges of conspiracy to traffic a drug of dependence
- 1 charge of possessing a drug of dependence

Sentence: 8 years

Patrizio 'Patty' CONDRO
- 3 charges of trafficking a drug of dependence
- 2 charges of conspiracy to traffic a drug of dependence
- 3 charges of possessing a drug of dependence

Sentence: 4 years

Vincenzo 'Jim' VENTRICE
- Conspiracy to traffic a drug of dependence (50 pounds of amphetamine)

Sentence: 3 years suspended

Six

July 29-31, 1992

When I was first finding my feet at the Drug Squad, good undercovers would often describe the job as being like a junkie's first rush of heroin. Once you got a taste, you chased it forever after. At that time, I thought they were full of shit, but even now I still remember the adrenaline rushes from Operation Bert. From that period onwards, I was hooked.

Roughly a fortnight after Bert wound up, word got back to me from the town of Mildura. Apparently a few locals had elevated me to hero status, so pronounced had been their fear of Medici and his drug buddies. Like a crazy-eyed kid, I lounged in the limelight that came my way.

Looking back, my swollen head was probably a good thing. If I had stopped and thought about what I'd just been through, I probably would've lost my nerve and never done another job. Better to annoy people with my puffed-up persona than to develop some sort of post-traumatic stress disorder.

Even so, there wasn't a whole lot of time to get too carried away with myself. Other minor jobs were in progress and, looking towards the horizon, I was positioning myself as a frontrunner for Operation Twin.

Twin's objectives were twofold. Firstly, local bikies were operating a chemist's of sorts out of a Lakes Entrance pub, selling a shitload of amphetamine and cannabis. By all

Undercover

accounts they weren't being all that discreet about their trade. Understandably the town's coppers were getting jack of it, and we were their final port of call. Every other strategy had failed.

The second component of Twin took us about an hour or two east of Lakes Entrance. The Gippsland towns of Orbost and Club Terrace were being used as bases for local marijuana growers. Intelligence led us to believe that several clandestine crops were yielding massive amounts of cannabis in the area.

On the surface, I liked the sound of it. I only had to consider the operation's perks: months of fun in the winter sun at a seaside location with a beautiful partner (Kim Culpin) to work alongside.

When I was given the green light to hit the Princes Highway with Kim a few weeks later, I was more excited than Patty Condro juggling a couple of pies at lunchtime.

Lakes Entrance is about a four-hour drive from Melbourne, taking in the towns of Traralgon, Sale and Bairnsdale along the way. Nowadays the Princes Highway's a quiet affair, although it is a bit of a magnet for the curious expecting coastal views. In truth, there's not much to gawk at until you descend into Lakes Entrance with its cliff-top vistas of deep blue coast.

On July 29 we set up camp on the main drag at the Bamboo Motor Inn, and that night we set up shop in the front bar at the Club Hotel just down the road. Our cover story for the first part of Twin read this way: we were small-time amphetamine dealers looking to buy gear we could offload to others in the Gippsland area.

Posing as boyfriend and girlfriend, we drank some beer, shot some pool, talked some shit, and made ourselves out to be the most approachable party people in the shire. Once we gained some trust, the plan was to buy drugs from anyone who offered them, and then on bust day lock up the whole town, so to speak.

It wasn't easy at first. Like most country pubs, the Club Hotel didn't attract the most friendly of clientele. And when the clientele's a bunch of hostile bikies, you have to work twice as hard on your repertoire.

Luckily we had Kim as our bait. She was blonde, athletic, a bit of a tomboy. You could just tell that every bikie was dying to get into her pants. When she wasn't taking advances from the great unwashed, we flirted with each other a fair bit. To be honest, I didn't need much encouragement. She was pretty hard to resist. I was enjoying being close to her, but it was also a tough gig on occasions. How can I put this? Much to my annoyance, Kim liked girls more than boys.

Attracting drug dealers who don't know you can be a bit of a skill. I always played the knockabout and, in a pub, people would often approach me just for a chat anyway. If you knew they were likely to be involved in the drug trade, the idea was to sort of slip a request into the conversation without sounding desperate or too eager. In other words, just let your words hang in the air for a while. They would usually come back to you at a later time if you played it that way. Once people are comfortable with you, it's human nature that they want to please.

By closing time we were already fully entrenched in a shout with a few bikies. It was hard work keeping up with their brainless patter, but we managed to score an invite back to their house for a party. Personally, I never enjoyed mixing it with these so-called tough guys. I mean, how could you take their bullshit seriously? Without the safety of numbers, I've always believed that bikies are little more than homeless mechanics.

And all that crap about the strength of the fraternal bikie code was overplayed. When coppers put pressure on them, bikies rolled over just like everyone else. In my sixteen years on the force, I only met two blokes who wouldn't talk when pushed. And they weren't bikies. The criminal code's a load of crap. Good crooks don't give statements, but everyone's partial to a little informing.

Still, an invite into their world was too much of a good opportunity to let pass. When we arrived at the house, twenty or thirty bikies were standing around the living room doing what bikies do — shaking their fat arses to Rose Tattoo, ZZ Top and AC/DC. Cans of beer were being downed, and plenty of dope was being smoked.

I was never a big pot smoker, and the prospect of sharing a joint with a bunch of rancid bikies was not the most appealing. They probably had germs that hadn't even been discovered yet. So when the joint headed my way, I was hesitant.

Taking drugs was certainly not a requirement of undercover work, and declining the offer wasn't something that could give my cover away. Plenty of dealers didn't do drugs. Most did, but some of the more successful ones were more likely not to dip into their own stash. And besides, I'd always been a control freak, and from what I'd heard marijuana ate away at your control like a teenager with the munchies.

My police training also gave me no practical marijuana usage tips. On the courses I'd attended, I'd never tested drugs to become familiar with the effects — although I suspect I could have if I'd wanted to. There were strong rumours that others on the undercover training course wanted first-hand knowledge of pot's effects, and were subsequently taken away for a puff.

Damian Marrett

However, it was never really an organised thing, and it didn't occur to me that I should get a handle on the drug. It just never interested me.

But tonight was different. In order to gain the trust of our two-wheeled Neanderthal friends, it would be rude to pass up the invitation. When the big bearded fellow parked on the living room floor to my right handed me his hand-rolled number, I took a few puffs.

I was already half-pissed from the pub, so I went into it cautiously. After the initial tokes, however, I was losing it by the second. When the dope came my way on its next revolution, I made like Bill Clinton and skipped the drawback part of the deal. By the third pass around, I was no longer upright. I was stretched out on the carpet, unable to smoke, unable to do much of anything.

'Kim, I'm scared. I can't move,' I managed to slip out to my partner to the left of me. I was struggling big time.

She laughed. 'Yeah, I'm paralysed too.'

'Yeah, but I'm actually a bit worried,' I said, *sans* laughter.

'So am I.' And she started giggling again. I don't think she understood the gravity of my words. Or the gravitational pull that had pinned me to the carpet.

'Look, as soon as my legs start working again we'd better think about going.'

'Okay,' she replied.

At that stage my greatest fear was all about the timing: if I was this wasted after a few drags, how rooted would I be in half an hour's time? I wasn't keen to find out.

I lay there paralysed for what felt like hours, but was probably only thirty minutes. In my state, Angry Anderson and Rose Tattoo were starting to sound like visionaries. The situation was made even worse by one of the bikies directing snide remarks towards me. I can't recall exactly what he said, but he was aggro without saying anything directly to my face. Maybe he wanted me out of the picture so he could crack onto my 'girlfriend'. I was worried that he might do something to Kim without me being able to lift a finger. But who knows? He may just have taken a dislike to me. It's been known to happen before.

Finally I managed to gather the strength to sit up again. I took a mouthful of VB to dampen my throat and tapped Kim on the thigh. 'Time to go.'

'Okay, just give me a minute.'

'Kim, I'm serious. It's now or never.'

Kim looked over at the grim reality that was her 'boyfriend'. She only needed one look to fully understand how shitfaced he had become — he was as grey as an overcast Melbourne day. A decision was made: she'd have to take him home.

'Hey, we're going,' she said, lifting me off the ground.

'Yeah,' I added. Was that me? It felt weird, like someone else was doing my talking for me.

A couple of grunts were fired back at us, and we managed to make it to the car outside for the trip back to the motel. Kim was driving.

'Were you freaking out?' I asked, sounding like a Sunbury survivor. 'Could you move?'

'A little bit,' she said, now on the highway. 'I reckon it was laced with something.'

'That was truly fucked up. They could've had their evil ways with us.'

'Don't you remember that part, Damian?'

By the time we arrived at our motel it was 3:30 a.m. and I was in desperate need of some sleep. Debriefing with our controller, Jim 'Bull' Pitt, was planned for seven the next morning at Metung, twenty minutes southeast of Lakes Entrance. Alarm clocks were alarmed, and I had a feeling I would be sleeping the sleep of ten tired men.

The next morning we struggled out of bed and made for Metung, and Bull. It hadn't been practical to wear wires the night before, so we had to recount every last detail of an evening that had more than enough sketchy details. Names of bikie members and the address of the party were passed on. It was also explained to Bull that we had built up quite a good rapport with most of them. Personally, I was pretty happy with myself: I managed to keep my eyes open for the whole of the debrief.

Later in the afternoon we made a move down the highway to Orbost. It was time to meet our farm boys, the Gippsland growers.

Our approach to the second component of Twin was a little more sophisticated than just lobbing up to the local pub. We planned on using a police informer, Gary Aldridge, to introduce us to the main players in the cannabis-growing community.

Gary Aldridge was a weasel of a man. In his mid-forties, his physical features and cunning were more rat than man. No matter the circumstance, he always scrubbed up the same — shoulder-length hair, stained singlet top and a pair of denims rolled up a good ten centimetres at the bottom. Even during the mid-eighties I'd never liked that look. In the mid-nineties it was ridiculous.

For the whole term of Operation Twin Aldridge thought I was a crook, just like he was. My identity as an undercover operative was never revealed to him. It was just another scheme cooked up by my boss, Detective Sergeant Jim Pitt.

Undercover

Getting a handle on the inner workings of Jim's mind would have been a psychiatrist's worst nightmare. I didn't know it at the time (or I was too naive to cotton on), but Bull was the master of the hidden agenda. The bloke was an innovator, a police officer who did his thinking outside the square. Actually, his mind never occupied the square in the first place.

At that time I liked Bull, but I was still very cautious of him. After leaving the force in the late nineties, he sadly fell foul of the law.

On Twin, Bull was banking on a convoluted plot that ran something like this ... First off, he introduced the informer Aldridge to a fellow undercover known only as Brian. Bull then proceeded to inform Aldridge that he was after a third party: me. I was then introduced to Aldridge through Brian under the premise that I was a crook who Bull was looking to put away. Are you still with me? I told you that Bull Pitt was one of a kind.

I guess Bull's motivation to play the operation in that fashion was a masterstroke. We suspected that Aldridge couldn't be trusted as an informer. If he dealt drugs to me, unaware that I was a copper, we could put him away as well as the others when the operation came to a conclusion. We could also keep tabs on him to see if he was upfront and, as a bonus, it was more than likely he would vouch for a fellow criminal, namely me, in front of his criminal mates. He didn't know it, but Gary Aldridge was being played from every angle.

So, for the Orbost part of the operation, Brian was my partner. The reason that we didn't use Kim Culpin was a simple one. Bikies are more likely to respond to a boyfriend–girlfriend drug-dealing team. It had already been established that they were naturally attracted to Kim. Most of them thought with their dicks anyway. Down the highway, though, the dope growers were a hardened bunch. A woman's place was in the kitchen or on her back. Well, that's how we read their approach.

That afternoon I met up with Aldridge at his little shack in Cann River. I was with Brian, a man who Aldridge knew as an undercover cop. He also thought that I was unaware of this, and there's no doubt that Aldridge felt confident that I was one of Operation Twin's targets, not him.

'Hi Gary,' Brian said in his lilt. 'This is the bloke I was telling you about.'

Just a little bit about Brian. Twin was one of his first undercover jobs, and one of his last as well. Nice bloke and a good friend, but Brian had a tendency to talk a bit too much. An Irish fella, he probably kissed the Blarney Stone one too many times. Sometimes when he was wound up, his conversation was also tinged with uncertainty. It pissed me off, because any time I tried to take a crook down a certain path, Brian would chip in with an observation about Gary Ablett's uncanny goal-scoring feats that was invariably wrong.

For purely selfish reasons, talking too much was also a bad habit to get into. 'Go easy on the talking, mate,' I remember telling Brian early on. 'You'll get the drift next week when you have to transcribe a hundred pages of bullshit.'

After wearing a wire, part of our job was transcription. One hour of dialogue equalled roughly four hours of hammering away at a keyboard. Undercover work became rather mundane when Brian was banging on about the footy for twenty minutes.

But back to Aldridge. After introductions, we got down to business. 'Brian said you might be able to hook me up with some green,' I said.

Undercover

'How much are you after?' asked Aldridge.

'A shitload.' No point in pussyfooting around. 'I hear you know some people with pretty big crops.'

'Yeah, yeah, yeah, I can put you onto the right people, no worries there.'

'I just wanna buy whatever I can 'cause I can get rid of it easy.'

'Yeah, well, if you never fuck me up with the money,' he said, 'you can have whatever you want.'

'No problems on that score,' I said. 'So when can I meet some of these blokes then?'

'Come down the pub. You never know your luck.'

We jumped into a Holden ute that was my car for the job. About twenty minutes west from Aldridge's digs was the Bellbird Hotel, in between Orbost and Cann River. An odd little country pub, it looked more like a three-bedroom weatherboard house than a drinking hole. Still, once you walked in the door it had a real welcoming feel to it, an open fireplace roaring away in the front bar.

I got the beers in, and scoped the room. Aldridge started chatting to a bloke who looked like Terence Hill from the Trinity movies. Kind of an obscure reference, but he was in his late thirties, fit, clean living, and clear-eyed. He looked like Gippsland's poster boy for healthy farm life.

This was John Dugdale, whose name Aldridge mentioned on the car ride to the pub. He had built him up to be one of the area's most consistent growers of large cannabis crops. John and his two brothers were known locally as the 'Madmen of Club Terrace', a town ten minutes north of the highway between Orbost and Cann River.

I always had a quiet chuckle to myself when Club Terrace was brought up in conversation. To me, it sounded more like a retirement village than a small Victorian country town. In reality, it was *Deliverance* country — half a dozen houses, everyone strumming banjos or whittling wood on their verandas. The Dugdales were the exception. They were out tending their cannabis crops and, by all accounts, sold garbage bags full of very good grass. John Dugdale was a target we needed on our books.

Brian and I stood by the Bellbird's bar while Aldridge talked to Dugdale. The dope grower was seated beside the fireplace looking like king shit. You could tell he wasn't the most approachable bloke. A few minutes later Aldridge introduced us, and I tried to strike up a conversation: 'Gary says you might be able to help me with some stuff.'

'Stuff? What fucking stuff?' Dugdale answered gruffly with an evil stare, one eye roughly twice the size of the other.

'Well, I'm after some green.'

The right eye was bulging out of his skull now. 'And why would you be asking me?'

'Gary just told me that you might be able to help me, but if you can't, you can't, you know,' I said. John Dugdale made you back-pedal even when you didn't want to.

'Don't know what you're talking about.' He picked up his beer and turned away to face the flame.

I took that as my cue to get out of there, walking back to the bar in order to bail up Aldridge.

'You've gotta be fucken jokin', Gary. He doesn't want a bar of us.'

'Don't worry. It'll be right. Him and his brothers are pricks to everyone.'

He wasn't wrong. The Dugdale brothers were widely known in the trade as Gippsland's surliest dope growers. They weren't called the 'Madmen of Club Terrace' for nothing. Even though they ran a thriving business churning out loads of dope every year, they'd never been known to crack a smile in mixed company.

John was the oldest of the three, an imposing and self-righteous fucker if ever I'd met one. They were making money hand over fist from marijuana, but hated their customers more than life itself. As such, John ran the family concern like some sort of crackpot crusader. If the Dugdales knew you liked a toke on a joint, you were a dole-bludging waste of space. Fair enough, but they'd created and cornered a market they had very little time for. I found it all a bit strange. Kind of like a restaurant owner who won't eat his own food, and can't stand his clientele. Like a McDonald's franchisee.

After finishing up our drinks, we made our way to the door. Dugdale was heading back to his throne by the fire after taking a slash. Our paths met, and he stopped me with a tap on my arm. 'I'll have two for you next week. See me down here.' Before I had a chance to firm up the price on two pounds of Dugdale dope, he was already warming his hands over the flames.

Okay, we had ourselves a dealer. Interesting way of doing business though.

Our next stop was Marshall's Commonwealth Hotel in Orbost. Marshall's was a handsome old corner pub with wooden balconies shadowing the main street. The front bar was full of men from Snowy River, knocking the froth off a couple after a hard day tending their fields, probably on horseback.

Aldridge told us that local grower Bill Hancock was a regular drinker at Marshall's. But when we arrived at the pub Bill was elsewhere, so we downed a quiet one before retiring for the evening.

Besides the Hancock no-show, things were travelling smoothly. Speed-dealing bikies from Lakes Entrance were beginning to trust us. The shifty Gary Aldridge thought I was a crook. In turn, he was introducing me to some of the biggest dope cultivators from Gippsland. And one of the best growers, angry prick John Dugdale, wanted to deal me two pounds of grass next week. It appeared that Twin was heading in the right direction.

The next night Kim and I were back at the Club Hotel for some more bikie action. Although it was a Friday, there wasn't much to report. They must have been off at a bikies' convention somewhere, plotting new and interesting ways of taking over a town with only the concerted swing of a bikie chain and a steely resolve. Or maybe it was weekly shower night. Who knew?

After a few games of pool, we were just about to call it a night when a conspicuous interloper lobbed through the door. This guy clearly didn't belong in the front bar of a bikie pub. Five minutes later, parts of the puzzle fell into place when a second conspicuous interloper waltzed in as well. Same body language, same clean-cut look, same immaculate level of hygiene. These guys were connected. Something was up.

You could just tell that we were about to be targeted. We already had this open persona to attract people, and we sure didn't look as threatening as some of the other scrotes necking beers in the bar. Even a monkey could've sensed that we were the friendliest people in the pub.

So it wasn't long before Mr Clean-cut's sordid little ruse was revealed. He approached us almost straightaway, about as naturally as his specialised covert training allowed. Yes, you didn't have to be a genius to work out that we had a fellow undercover on our hands. Probably a fed, a Federal policeman.

'Do ya know where I can get on, mate?' he asked, as nervy as a bloke on the cusp of a breakdown. What a piss-

Undercover

poor approach. Ten out of ten for the most clichéd opening in drug-dealing vernacular. This guy was a shocker.

'Just after a little taste, are you, mate?' I asked him.

'Yeah, yeah, can you get me on?' His eyes lit up. He had a target in his sights.

'Whaddya want?'

'Goey mate, goey. Can you get us on?' This was textbook stuff.

'I don't really sell Gs, mate. I can do you a pound though. Yeah?'

This was getting more and more exciting by the minute for our Federal Police brother. 'Yeah, yeah, a pound's good,' he replied.

The guy was a complete moron. His drug-buying technique just didn't add up at all. He's supposed to be a loser user wanting to get on, but then all of a sudden he's after a pound. It's like wanting to buy a shitty old Gemini for a couple of hundred, and then at the last minute deciding you'd prefer a Lamborghini for half a mill.

'What's your story, mate? Where are you from?' I could be a cruel bastard at times.

'Aah, er, Queensland.'

By this stage Kim was quietly pissing herself, but egging me on in the process. 'Well, help him out, Damian,' she said.

'I don't know. How do I fucken know who you are, buddy? How long have you been in Lakes Entrance? Who are you here with?'

A noticeable sweat started breaking out over his forehead. 'No one, mate. No one.'

'Who's that fucken bloke over there, then?' I pointed to his minder sitting over a pot of beer in the corner.

Under interrogation, Mr Clean-cut wasn't holding up too well. If I'd been a crook, I would've belted him by now.

On top of that, he didn't even bother to look over at his mate after I'd pointed him out. 'Don't know, don't know. I'm by myself, mate. I just want to get on, ya know.'

'All right, mate, I don't know why I'm doing this, but we can sell you a pound.'

'Nice one, yeah. How much?'

'Twenty-five a pound.' The price set at $25 000 a pound was clearly stretching it, but I had a feeling he wouldn't be bargain-hunting.

'No problems. When?'

'Tonight. Midnight. Do you know the old Lake Road?' I asked.

'Um, no. Yeah. I can find out.'

'Lake Road's about three Ks up the highway thataway,' I said, pointing east. 'Okay, there's a roundabout halfway up the road. Go round it twice. Just in case someone's tailing you. I'll be at the top of the second hill with the gear. No guns, okay?'

'No guns, nup, okay. Second roundabout?'

'No. Second hill. First roundabout. Two times. No guns.'

'Okay, okay, see ya there.'

And with that, he made a controlled dash for the door. Five minutes later, his mate was on the move as well. They had three hours to organise $25 000 for a buy/bust on a road that was a figment of my heartless imagination.

An hour later, Jim Pitt popped his head in at the local police station. The feds were all buzzing about these local drug dealers. There were descriptions of these two lowlife villains on a whiteboard, one male, one not. Bull was seconded to take a look to see if he could put a name to the details. He was afraid he could.

Understandably it didn't go down too well. The feds' operation was a fizzer.

Seven

August-December, 1992

The Lakes Entrance police station was in mourning on August 8, 1992. One of the coppers' daughters owned a horse. She loved that pony. The night before, some insensitive bastard had run it over on the road to Metung and left it for dead. The local vet had fortunately managed to save its life, but there would be no more showjumping for Trigger at the local gymkhana.

I should know. That insensitive bastard was me.

The night started off innocently enough. A few too many beers at the Club Hotel, plenty of talk about future speed deals with our biker boy mates Mick, Ben and Stretch, and even a bit of a dance with Kim at the Central Hotel disco afterwards.

Once the night wound down, we had to dash back to Metung for a debrief with Bull about the night's proceedings. On the road to his rented serviced apartment, tragedy struck.

I was driving the ute when out of the darkness came a black flash. Bloody Trigger. The horse hit the side of the bonnet, and the impact broke the driver's-side mirror. We came to a screaming halt, both jumping out of the car to look for the injured horse. It was black outside, and we couldn't see it anywhere. We took this as a good sign. Maybe it had managed to trot away.

Standing on the side of the road trying to work out where in the fuck Trigger had got to, we suddenly caught an image of some blue lights approaching from about a kilometre behind. Coppers. Because we had drugs in the car and didn't want to blow our covers, we thought it best to keep on the move, so I hot-tailed it to Metung and the safety of Bull's apartment. No worries. After the debriefing, we drove back to the Bamboo Motor Inn for some shuteye.

The next day we received word from the morgue that was the Lakes Entrance police station. The news wasn't good. Trigger would never negotiate the fences again. We felt like a couple of shits, but the good news was that the neddy wasn't destined for a dog bowl. It just needed plenty of R and R.

Anyway, sorry about that, little girl with an injured pony.

Gimpy showjumpers aside, things were hotting up on the drug-dealing front in Gippsland. Some of the larger deals for the months of August through November included:

- Two pound cannabis purchase ($4000) from John Dugdale at the Bellbird Hotel in Cann River.
- Two pound cannabis purchase ($4000) from Bill Hancock at Marshall's Hotel in Orbost.
- Two ounce amphetamines purchase ($3000) from Gary Aldridge at the Black Swan Motor Inn in Lakes Entrance.

Bull had been right about Aldridge. The deals our informer was doing with me were not going through our books. Instead of being a good little gig, he was playing both sides off against one another. In other words, the man was informing, but also secretly dealing drugs to us behind our backs.

He was also becoming something of a liability. On the stretch of highway between Orbost and Lakes Entrance, Gary Aldridge almost screwed everything up royally.

Undercover

I was barrelling the ute along the road when I was suddenly pulled over by a Traffic Operations Group copper (toggie). Aldridge was sitting beside me in the passenger seat. Underneath his feet was more than a pound of grass. A pistol was lying beneath my seat. Here's hoping we were looking at a speeding ticket without any added grief.

'Just wait there, Gary,' I said. 'I'll sort this out.'

I stepped out of the car, and walked over towards the toggie. He looked like a normal country copper, big and rugged, the obligatory moustache dangling over his top lip.

'Got your licence?' he asked.

I handed him some fake ID, explaining that my licence was at home.

'State your full name and address, then.'

No worries. I knew that one. I was Damon Bird of Flat 4, 37 O'Grady Street, Clifton Hill.

'What business have you got up here?'

'I'm a plumber,' I said, gesturing towards my ute. 'I've just come up to see some mates. Why? What's your problem?'

From out of nowhere, he slapped me fair and square across the right side of my face. Open hand, plenty of heat on it. Enough to make my face tingle anyway. I stood there grimacing, prepared to take my medicine for the time being.

'Bloody smartarse. I don't like cheeky cunts,' he said. 'Go sit in the car with your mate, and I'll be back.'

This was not looking too flash. It was as if he knew I was up to no good, and at that stage I thought he was going to search the car for sure. If he searched the car, my cover could be blown. At the very least, it would be a major pain in the arse. If I was 'arrested', word would spread quickly among local crooks. When you're arrested, without fail, suspicions are quickly raised. You know, 'Did he do a deal with the coppers? I heard that he turned on us to get bail.' The criminal world thrives on gossip, and if I was hauled into the local station, my name would be mud until proven otherwise.

Still, I timidly scuffed back to a waiting Aldridge, who'd just seen the lot through the rear-view mirror.

'Fucken arsehole,' he said. 'You oughta just pop him one, mate.'

By 'pop' he wasn't indicating I should throw on a cassette of Michael Jackson tunes and moonwalk the prick to death.

'Nah, nah, let's just see how it plays out.'

'Look at him, mate,' Aldridge said, peering into the passenger's-side mirror. 'We could just pop him and drive away.'

I turned around. The toggie had his foot on the bumper bar at the back of his car. He was talking into a radio in his hand and, worst of all, he had his back to us. If I'd been of a mind to shoot him, it would be an ideal time and place. The road was deserted and his back was a fair target area.

'Just fucken shut up, will ya, Gary?' I was getting annoyed. 'There's fucken nothing in it.'

'Yeah mate, I know. I'm just saying, that's all.'

Aldridge was probably right though. There's no way a cop should turn his back on someone under suspicion. Turning your back on *anyone* when you're in uniform is a dangerous game.

A minute or two later the cop came back to my window and handed me back my ID without a word. He then did a slow circuit of the car, stopping briefly at the rear. 'I'm giving you a ticket,' he said, scribbling away. 'You've got a towbar over your numberplate. Get it fixed.'

Undercover

With that he turned his back on us, marched to his car and a minute later sped off, no wiser. The whole episode was over. I was home free. And so were the toggie and Gary Aldridge.

'What a dumb fucker,' said Aldridge, picking up the bag of grass and tossing it in the air for fun.

'You're telling me,' I laughed. Jesus Christ. What sort of coppers do they breed in the bush? If he'd had any suspicions whatsoever, he should've searched the car. And yeah, thanks for the slap, bitch.

Never underestimate the sheer stupidity of certain crooks. Operation Bert's Patty Condro was a prime example. The normally switched-on Bill Hancock was another.

Hancock's three great passions in life were horse racing, fishing, and growing acres and acres of female cannabis plants — the most potent form of marijuana. Male plants were all leaf and stem. To most people around him, he appeared to be a hard-working farmer. To others of a particular bent, he was a respected expert on all things marijuana.

He also had a bit of respect from local coppers. One night there was a big blue at the Marlo pub, and Bill jumped in to save the good guys. Apparently he held off four blokes. Well, that's what I've been told, and he was pretty tough for an old fella. In fact, he copped a bit of flak for the whole episode in criminal circles.

To be honest, I have no beef with the man. If he hadn't been a drug dealer, I probably would've considered him a mate. He could be a decent enough bloke, and even cluey and likeable at times. But sometimes he'd just spin you out with his homespun hokum when it came to police surveillance procedures.

Damian Marrett

One day we were in the front bar of Marshall's Hotel talking about what can and can't be picked up by police detection.

'You've always got to be careful talking outside, you know,' he said, his big right hand cradling a pot of beer.

'What? It's much better outside, Bill. The walls have ears,' I said.

'Mate, never talk outside, because they've got this plane that's so far up in the sky you can't even see it. They've got a deaf sheila up there with a telescope who reads lips. They go *that* far.'

Hmmm.

Some of the stories you'd hear from crooks about what they thought cops were capable of used to floor me. Most of them were just clueless, but I wasn't going to get into a shitfight with Bill Hancock about the finer points of police surveillance. Let him work it out for himself.

While Twin was occupying a lot of my time, other buy/busts with less involved levels of infiltration also demanded attention. That was the thing about undercover work: you could never concentrate fully on just the one job. In the morning you could be buying ounces of powders posing as a crook called Ben Cross, and then you'd have to back up in the afternoon as a hitman known only as Rick Clyde. When you weren't on your guard, it had the potential to confuse.

I recall one time I was doing four jobs at once. Not only four different jobs, but also four different identities. My mobile phone rang in the middle of the night after I'd gone to bed half-pissed. On the third ring, I picked it up.

'Hello,' I murmured, neither asleep nor awake.

'Sorry to ring so late, mate,' a voice said, 'but I've got some gear for you tomorrow.'

'Yeah, okay.' I had no idea who was on the other end. Shit, I had no idea who I was at this end.

'I finally got onto my bloke, so sorry about the delay,' the voice continued.

'Ah, that's great.' Still no idea.

'So I'll meet you at the usual place tomorrow, yeah?'

'What time?' I asked, stifling a yawn. No matter who I was, I always liked to be punctual. Even when I didn't know where I was going.

'Better make it three,' he laughed. 'You sound like you'll be sleeping in late.'

I yawned now. To hell with the stifling. The truth be known, I was just trying to fire up my brain, wondering where I could take this conversation next. 'Yeah mate, you caught me at a funny time. It'll be good stuff, right?'

'Yeah, good shit, good price,' he said.

I needed more information. 'Shit' could be anything. 'Are you sure it's good?'

'Yeah, why wouldn't it be? It's straight from the lab, still moist.'

Amphetamines. Sorted. It was Paul Price, my powders man, the target of Operation Sahara.

'Sounds good, no worries, Pricey,' I said. 'See you at the Black Prince about three then.'

Around the time of Twin, one buy/bust that required my time and effort was codenamed Operation Spot. It involved a Kiwi drug dealer, Jason Anderson. His name popped up in a conversation with an informer we had in our care. This gig was confident that Anderson was capable of dealing hundreds, possibly thousands of ecstasy pills.

Wired for sound, I first met Anderson on the southern bank of the Yarra River, directly opposite the Nylex clock. He was a trendy-looking bloke kitted out in black jeans and T-shirt, a studded belt buckle planted on his hips. The early nineties was a strange time. The long-haired Anderson had probably been a rock pig only months earlier, but now that ecstasy was so much in demand, techno was his thang. Es go better with techno, and most of his evenings were spent at inner-city clubs and raves, supplying the patrons with party drugs.

At that first meeting the informer was tagging along to provide an introduction, but I'd told him beforehand to nick off after five minutes. So after a few early exchanges feeling each other out, the informer made his apologies, and only then did the two of us really start talking drugs.

'Can you get your hands on trips too?' I asked.

In 1992, LSD was making a huge comeback after screwing up hippies twenty years before. Blame the rave culture for its repeat showing. If you could drop acid for twenty, twenty-five bucks, why bother coughing up fifty or sixty for a tab of E? Sure, it was cheaper but, in my experience from observing rather than indulging, LSD's effects were much more damaging and far-reaching.

Dealers loved acid too. The risks associated with trafficking the drug were trifling. If you were importing 100 000 tickets, they could easily be stashed away amongst documents in a small package. LSD was odourless, and if customs didn't open up the package (and they had no good reason to when the sniffer dogs passed it by), you were home free. Even X-rays couldn't pick up the stuff.

'Sure. The Daffy Ducks are going right off,' he replied. At that time there were batches of LSD tickets with Warner Brothers cartoon characters on them. Tweety Bird, Bugs Bunny and Elmer Fudd had also been immortalised.

'Yeah, I've heard that.'

'Mate, I can get you some, no problems.'

'How much?'

'Nine bucks each,' he said. 'But only if you buy more than a thousand.'

'And the Es?'

'Bloody good stuff, you know the doves,' he said, referring to a popular pill that was stamped with a small peace dove. 'They're the same deal with the minimum, but they're twenty each.'

'I'm just looking to get as much as I can get my hands on, you know, especially the acid. When can you get us some samples?'

'Whenever. Just call my pager when you're ready.'

A day later I paged Anderson, and he got straight back to me on the hello phone at the Russell Street office. A few hours later I rocked up to the same spot on the Yarra. Anderson was already waiting for me, casually stretched out on the grass.

'Mate, I've got five of each,' he said. 'You can have them for a hundred.'

I looked around furtively, just like a drug dealer would before he pulled a $100 note out of his pocket, and the five LSD tickets and five ecstasy tabs were mine.

'Great. Oh yeah, I nearly forgot. I can get my hands on chemicals,' I said. 'You know anyone who'd want some red phosphorous?'

Red phosphorous is a hard-to-get component that goes into the making of amphetamines. I had three reasons for bringing this up: firstly, I wanted to find out if Anderson was dealing speed as well; secondly, it was a great way of diverting suspicion — if you're trying to offload gear at the same time as buy it, a target's more likely to feel comfortable and trust you; and thirdly, there could be a chance that my inquiries would lead to a manufacturer and supplier.

'Maybe,' he replied. 'I'll get in touch with a bloke I know. You know I can get you goey as well, don't you?'

'Yeah? I might be interested in that. I'll speak to my man about it.'

'You want ounces?'

'Can you get hold of a pound?' I asked.

'That shouldn't be a problem.'

'How much?' I asked.

'It's 35 000 a pound.'

'Shit. Bloody steep.'

'Nah, this stuff's really good, pure shit. It's worth every cent,' he spruiked.

Three days later, I contacted him and organised a deal. 'Mate, I'll take a thousand of the round ones, and five thousand of the papers, okay?'

'What about the other stuff?'

'Um, are you sure it's that good?'

'Mate, the quality will blow you away, no bullshit. You can go seven to one on it.' What he meant was that after cutting it with glucose and the like I'd have eight pounds of the stuff, not just the one.

'What's your best price then?'

'Look mate, if you get all the other stuff, how's thirty-one sound?'

'You've sold me,' I said. 'Put us down for one.'

I then organised to meet him in the car park of the Denny's Restaurant on the corner of the Nepean Highway and North Road in East Brighton at nine o'clock that night. It was a good location for a buy/bust — secluded, with excellent access points when coppers were in a hurry.

The buy was then set for 5000 LSD tickets at $9 a pop, one pound of speed at $31 000, and 1000 tabs of ecstasy at

$20 each. The grand total for less than a week's worth of infiltration was $96 000.

As planned, Anderson was at the purchase site right on the knocker of nine. I was waiting for him in a blue Commodore he'd already seen me driving at our previous meetings.

'How's things, mate?' he asked, stepping into the passenger seat.

'Good, good, Jason. Ready to go?'

'Here's the acid,' he said, passing me a Manila folder. I opened it up. Inside were ten or so sheets of detachable LSD tabs, Daffy Duck's little face smiling up at me 5000 times.

Anderson then told me he had a contact in Amsterdam who could send through tickets in lots of 50 000. He reckoned he could beat this Dutchman down to $3 a ticket. Did I want to get involved in a joint venture? I told him I'd think about it, but we still had business to conduct.

'Where's the rest?' I asked.

'I can get the speed here in five minutes, but I've gotta travel for the Es.'

'Whaddya mean by travel?'

'Well, if you give us the twenty grand, I'll take off, grab the gear, and be back in half an hour.'

'You've gotta be joking,' I sneered. 'You said that you'd have it all here.'

'Yeah, I know, but I didn't have enough time.'

For the next five minutes we argued about the situation. There was no way I was going to let the money run. He then said he was prepared to give me his passport as trust. I said I'd need a little more insurance than a New Zealand passport. I mean, come on! If you were a Kiwi, you'd be trying to renounce the bloody thing anyway.

In the meantime, I got him to ring through the speed. Five minutes later, a cab pulled into the car park, and Anderson hopped out of the car to meet his courier.

When he was out of earshot I talked out of the side of my mouth for the benefit of the listening and recording devices. 'A taxi has just pulled into the car park. Anderson's just taken possession of a small box from a bloke in a green baseball cap. That's a green baseball cap and blue T-shirt.'

I knew that someone would intercept the cab after it left the car park, but in the meantime Anderson made his way back to the Commodore. He then handed over the box and its contents. Inside was a clear plastic bag chock-a-block with white powder.

'There's your pound, mate,' he said. 'Oh yeah, and that red phosphorous of yours — I know a bloke who might be interested in it.'

'That bloke just then?' I asked, meaning the courier in the taxi.

'Nah, another bloke.'

'Beauty. Just ask him how much he wants, and we'll take it from there.'

'No worries. You got the money then?'

I had to pay Anderson for the LSD and amphetamine, but I wasn't letting him take some money to get the ecstasy. I could feel a bust coming on.

'Yeah, it's in the boot. I'll just get it out. Googa will be happy with this,' I said, tapping the box. Once again, Googa's name was our bust signal. I then left the box on my seat, and got out of the car to fish the money from the boot. Before I had a chance to sling the backpack of cash on my shoulder and return to the vehicle's interior, the SOG boys did their thing, screeching in from all angles and surrounding the car.

It was quite a sound and sight spectacular. Anderson was apprehended without so much as a peep, and I was cleaned up by one of the SOG tough guys, Damien. He then proceeded to stick the boots into my midriff. He was actually kicking the gun that was down my pants, and the force of his foot was driving the gun's barrel down into my balls. It was bloody killing me.

'Give it a rest, will ya?' I shrieked.

'Shut the fuck up, scumbag,' he replied, convinced that I was putting on a show for Anderson's benefit. That was the problem when I was arrested with all the others in a buy/bust: my SOG colleagues were hellbent on 'keeping it real', often treating me with far more vigour than the crooks themselves.

I looked up at Damien with hope more than anything else, but he was having none of it, tapping me with his foot a couple of more times. The pain was excruciating, but I had no choice other than to deal with the gun-in-the-gonads scenario in silence.

When I had a chance, I lifted my head to see what else was going on. All I could see were dozens of shocked faces pressed up against Denny's windows. They'd come to the restaurant for a good cheap meal; the show outside was a freebie.

Fifteen minutes later, when Googa and I were driving out of the car park after a job well done, a Volvo sedan pulled up beside us. The businessman driving it motioned for us to wind down our window. It looked like he wanted to tell us something.

'Mate, I just saw what happened from the restaurant,' he said, pointing back at Denny's. 'I've gotta say, you blokes have got balls of steel.'

'No worries, mate,' I said, a bit embarrassed by his call.

Damian Marrett

We took off again, one hand nursing my crotch. I could've done with a set of those steel balls fifteen minutes ago.

Christmas Day 1992, and I was in Melbourne for a family gathering. Very pleasant, but the next day promised to be a little less relaxing. I'd organised a meeting with Gary Aldridge. He'd promised me a night-time drive to let us have a stickybeak at one of the crops in the backblocks near Club Terrace. It was supposedly massive, well hidden, and booby-trapped. Although Aldridge refused to tell us who it belonged to, we suspected the Dugdales had a hand in it.

The Victoria Police Drug Squad was very keen to put this particular crop under surveillance. I'd already put out the word that I wanted to buy hundreds of pounds from the Dugdales, so it was only natural that I should check out my investment. Over the last few months I'd been pushing Aldridge pretty hard, meeting after meeting, for a private viewing.

He had also promised that we'd meet the blokes who looked after the crop, but they'd stuck two conditions on our visit: the trip could only be done at night, and my car would be checked for wires or devices. Aldridge made a point of saying that they'd sweep the car when we arrived.

On Christmas Eve I'd relayed this information to the bosses in one of the corridors at Russell Street. 'What? They want to sweep the car?' one of them asked.

'Yep.'

'Is it a hire car?'

'Yep.'

'No way. Nup, no way,' he said. 'You'll need a tracking device, because if something happens to you and they knock off that car, we won't be able to find it. We've still gotta pay for it. By the day.'

The two other bosses' jaws hit the carpeted floor. From what I could gather, it appeared that the health of a hire car was seemingly more important than the health of an operative. *When big money's on the line, you don't fuck with the budget, Damian.* That was the mentality.

'Look, I'll leave a little note with my mum,' I said. 'If they get away with the hire car after knocking me, you can take it out of my police payout.'

When I put it that way, an apology was forthcoming.

Even so, when it came to back up for this little midnight rendezvous, there appeared to be a dilemma. We couldn't rely on cover cars (unmarked police cars in the vicinity) because we had no idea where Aldridge was taking me in the first place. This is why we were so keen to put a tracker on the car. But, tracker or no tracker, this was a cracking opportunity too good to pass up.

Boxing Day, and we loaded up the hire car (charged at a daily rate) for the drive east to Lakes Entrance. Jim Pitt and two other detectives came along for the ride. After dumping our gear at the motel, I hooked up with Gary Aldridge at 7 p.m. We pissfarted around for a few hours and then, at about ten-thirty, it was time to check out this crop.

Ten minutes into our drive, Aldridge pulled a swifty. 'Oh yeah, I forgot to tell ya — the blokes aren't gonna meet us.'

'The blokes who run the crop?' I asked, knowing the reply would be bad news. Could've bloody used a tracker.

'Yeah.'

'Why?' I asked.

'Don't know, but I know where it is anyway. They just don't want anyone to take look at the crop.'

Damian Marrett

I then understood that we were making this visit without the caretakers' permission. There was no need for me to ask the question.

Shooting down the Princes Highway, Aldridge directed me to take a left at the turn-off for Lind National Park and Club Terrace. I did as he requested, but I noticed a distinct change in his behaviour the closer we got to the crop. The whole thing was quite bizarre. He became nervous, and I had no understanding of why.

After passing through Club Terrace, we drove another 10 kilometres down the road. Aldridge then instructed me to pull the car over. It appeared we had reached our destination.

'Rightio, let's go take a look then,' I said, reaching for the door.

'Nah, I'm not going in there,' he replied.

'Whaddya mean?' I asked, sitting tight, no longer reaching for the door.

'I'm just not going in there, okay? You can go by yourself. Just walk that way for about a hundred metres,' he said, pointing towards the right-hand side of the road.

'Come on. Come with me.'

'If you walk in a straight line, you should be right,' he said, beginning to look even more apprehensive than five minutes ago. 'I reckon it's only about one hundred metres, I don't know, maybe two.'

'Don't be fucken gutless, Gary. What are you afraid of?'

'Nothing. You go. Just be careful of booby traps.'

Thanks for the reminder. Booby traps on illegal crops are standard issue throughout Australia. A common method to deter nosy arseholes like me is to attach tripwires to loaded shotguns. When you trigger it, obviously a fair bit of damage can be done, and it goes without saying that I didn't want my balls blown off. Crop growers also use fishing hooks which get stuck in your hands when you brush aside plants that are in your way. To be honest, I'd much prefer that method of persuasion to get the fuck off their property.

Not only that, the crops were sure to be well concealed. Even large clusters on the wide expanses of Crown land are difficult to locate and, as a rule, plantations are grown amongst taller bushes, making them almost impossible to identify from the air. At night, in total darkness, I knew I would struggle. Most plantations were found by accident rather than by design.

'Well, at least get out of the car then,' I said.

'Nah, I'm okay here. Go for it. You were the one who wanted to see it.'

He had a point, but he was still weirding me out. Here I was, in the middle of bloody nowhere with a crook/informer who definitely couldn't be trusted. He'd proven it by dealing drugs to me, and not reporting the fact to my superiors. Not only that, snipers in the area were also a very real possibility, booby traps were probably just itching to get a hold of me or blow my head off, and to top it all off, the closest police presence was about two hours away. I wasn't painting a pretty picture for myself, and this had all the hallmarks of a set-up.

I then recalled that, on Christmas Eve, the bosses had even told me that I didn't have to go through with this expedition if I didn't want to. I'd been given an out clause and it hadn't even crossed my mind to take it. Don't get me wrong — I'm no tough guy. But my stupid pride meant that I could never back down, even when I knew that bad shit was about to happen to me. Nice one, idiot!

I stepped out of the car, putting both hands in my pockets. One hand enveloped a yellow plastic object. At least I had my GPS to keep me company.

Damian Marrett

The Global Positioning System (GPS) would give us a handle on where this crop was located. So, even without the tracker, we'd have a fair idea where the marijuana was supposed to be. At a later stage, we'd definitely be back for another squiz.

The first thing I noticed when I got out of the car was nothing. And plenty of it. The sky was deathly black on a starless and moonless night. I could only just make out my feet as I walked off to the side of the road. All I knew was that everything ahead of me was black and bushy. I also had concerns about the terrain. The road to Club Terrace was quite hilly, one side of it virtually vertical. I was hoping that the land levelled out somewhat after the town. Flat terrain would be good. A cliff-top would be bad.

As soon as I left the road, and Aldridge's sight, I pulled out my gun for protection. There was no need beforehand to show him I was carrying a pistol. If I started waving the thing around in company, word would spread quickly. I didn't want to up the ante on this operation. Once you start showing crooks that you're prepared to arm yourself, everyone tools up, sometimes for the most innocuous of reasons. Weddings, parties, future drug deals, anything.

I continued to walk into the bush, but still couldn't see a thing. Thankfully, the ground was sure under foot, but the whole scenario was ridiculous. After 15 or 20 metres, I pretty much gave up the ghost. Not only was my vision completely nonexistent, the foliage was close to impenetrable. Aldridge could've slapped a blindfold on me, and I'd have been just as useless negotiating the landscape. Unless I came back during daylight hours, there wasn't much hope of distinguishing tea tree from cannabis.

So I came to a decision: I'd gone far enough. I set the GPS, and set it again just in case. Although it was pitch

Undercover

black, I wrote down the numbers on a piece of paper as well. You can't be too careful.

I then sat there on the dirt for another five minutes, and lit up a smoke. Sat back and didn't move. The air around me was very still, and I couldn't hear a thing. I just tried to relax without thinking about someone wanting to jump me. After butting out the smoke, I walked the same path the other way, back to the road and Aldridge.

When I made it out, he did a kind of double take. Or did I imagine him doing one? Either way, I sensed he was surprised, maybe even shocked, that I was back in the car in one piece. I don't know though. The whole incident had spooked me a bit.

'That was a joke, right? Couldn't see a fucken thing,' I said, parking myself back in the driver's seat.

'What, nothing?'

'Just thick bush,' I said. 'I'm telling you, there's nothing there.'

'Go back in. It's fucken there. How far did you go in?' he asked.

'Far enough. Look, how about we come back tomorrow when it's daylight?'

'No fucken way. They'll shoot ya on sight.'

'What times are they here then?' I asked.

'All the time during the day. You'd be mad to come back.'

'It can't hurt asking. Give them a call tomorrow,' I said.

Aldridge didn't even bother answering, so I let it slide. Personally I didn't think there was a crop there at all. But why had he gone to such lengths to convince me otherwise? If I got lucky, maybe I'd find out at the end of the job.

Eight

January–April, 1993

Talking too much comes naturally to some people. Transcribing it doesn't. Most of January, I was glued to my Russell Street desk listening to Brian not drawing breath on a wire. Insignificant meetings quickly turned into 100-page opuses, and to top it all off, potential drug purchases were rarely, if ever, mentioned.

Despite all this, I was up to date on eastern Victoria's weather patterns (wettest summer since 1957, apparently), and I was fast becoming a recognised expert on crop fertilisation techniques. I could also point you in the right direction if you were looking to bag a brown trout in the area.

Furthermore, there were plenty of fiery front bar debates over who grew the best dope. In one corner, the open-air boys; in the other, the hydroponic upstarts. For hours on end, the Bill Hancocks of this world would defend to the death the great Gippsland dirt underneath their Blunnies.

Rightly or wrongly, Hancock believed that marijuana grown hydroponically lacked the strength of his gear: 'Yeah, yeah, it looks good and all,' he'd grumble over a pot of Carlton at Marshall's Hotel in Orbost, 'but it hasn't got the go in it.'

Of course the hydro boys felt slighted, counterclaiming that growing grass outdoors increased your chance of police exposure. They were also of the opinion that open-air crops required more maintenance and staff then their indoor operations.

Hancock would have none of it. The expense of hydro (equipment, electricity, pipe work, pumps, exhaust systems, etc.) far outweighed his outdoor operation. He also didn't like the limited crop size, and the fact that hydro properties had a name on the lease — most outdoor crops were on Crown land, playing havoc with prosecution.

I learned to keep my trap shut during these shitfights. Didn't want to mention that lip-reading deaf sheila and ruin Bill's argument.

Still, from a police point of view, surveillance was easier with indoor crops. Our helicopters were equipped with infrared tracking, sensing unnatural heat sources in buildings. Another big negative was that professional hydro crops were generally located in huge warehouses on industrial estates. The stench tended to waft into neighbours' nostrils. The very best exhaust system was a necessity, if not always foolproof.

While these arguments raged on and on, I also picked up way too much information about Hancock's life. He had problems with deer and possums eating his dope crop. Even rogue chooks liked to get on the gear. He owned a racehorse that looked like being a good thing if it could just get its barrier starts right. And back in 1975, he chopped off one of his toes for the compo. Three grand had been the going rate.

Yep, feigning interest in listless anecdotes is an occupational hazard for any working undercover. For instance, Bill Hancock loved fishing. I couldn't have given two shits about it. But if you'd sat in on one of our front bar conversations, you'd have thought I was hanging out to hear every ten-pound trout story that spewed out of his mouth.

Drug dealers beware: if people start listening intently to your boring stories, they could be working undercovers.

While we were mixing it with the crooks over a beer, I was trying to get my hands on a huge combined deal with Hancock and the Dugdales. I wanted 500 pounds of their crops.

Meanwhile, in Lakes Entrance, our inquiries with the bikies were running smoothly. Kim and I had no problems purchasing ounce deals of speed off them, and the bigger dealers in town had been identified. We had more than enough evidence on a dozen of them to make arrests when the time was right.

In the meantime, Gary Aldridge was prepared to deal largish quantities of amphetamines to me. Back in Melbourne, we met at the New Orleans Hotel in South Yarra. I had instructed him to hunt down amphetamines, a lot more than the three ounces I'd bought off him previously. Over the course of a few drinks, he mentioned that he might be able to get his hands on ten pounds of speed. I told him that I was prepared to part with $140 000 if he did.

Of course, in his role as an informer, none of this information was being relayed to Bull Pitt. Gary was enjoying these deals on the side too much, and informing for the cops was also proving to be a nice little earner.

Still, after half a dozen meetings Aldridge was struggling to come up with the ten pounds. He needed more time, but it appeared as though the volume was beyond his capabilities. By the time March rolled around, he told me that he was a month away from tying up the deal. We didn't have that much time to wait around, so close to our buy/bust opportunity. I was disappointed, but I kept a toe in the water all the same.

Brian and I went east again mid-March, trying to firm up amounts and prices in the front bar of Marshall's Hotel in Orbost. The 500-pound cannabis deal was still on the table. Meeting us was Bill Hancock and a bodybuilding lump of a man, the appropriately named Graham Strong, standing in for John Dugdale.

'Are you gonna tell them the bad news?' Hancock motioned to Strong.

'Um, you're not gonna like this, Damian, but John and the boys sold theirs a couple of weeks ago,' said Strong. 'It's all gone.'

'What? They've got nothing left?' I asked.

Hancock looked at Strong then at me. 'Well, you never know. You can't always believe what they say.'

'So you reckon he could be bullshitting?' I asked Strong.

'Look, I don't think so,' he replied. 'I reckon most of it's gone.'

'Shit. But it shouldn't affect the amount we talked about, right?'

'Yeah,' said Hancock, 'yeah it does.'

'It does?'

''Cause that was a big part of it,' Hancock explained.

'Okay, so, how much are we down?'

'Well, there'd be two lots. There'd be one ready first, and then one a month later,' said Strong. 'It's the only way we can do it, you know, bloody drying this stuff.'

Strong was alluding to the unseasonally wet weather Gippsland was experiencing. It was playing havoc with marijuana cultivation, and from a logistical point of view, crops were constantly being delayed because of the rain. Once the boys unearthed their loot, they spent days frantically trying to dry out the stuff. It buggered up our plans as well. Once again, our targets wouldn't deal all the gear in one hit. They wanted to drip-feed us.

'We'll probably be able to scrounge up two hundred,' Hancock chimed in.

'In two lots,' Strong repeated. 'Sorry mate, but John's like the wind.'

Quite rightly, I was pissed off. This was fast becoming a carbon copy of the Bert operation. And, yet again, the pressure was on me to negotiate one big deal for the buy/bust. Enough money had been let run. Budgets were as tight as always, and we didn't have another year to nail these blokes.

But, unlike Bert, I felt like I had gained the targets' complete confidence. For eight months I'd been saying all the right things, buying at all the right times. Although I was a newish player on the scene, I could tell I was trusted, and I was sure that Hancock and Strong weren't just trying to cover their arses in case I was a cop.

On the other hand, the timing wasn't so spectacular. At that stage, Hancock was becoming increasingly paranoid about his chosen occupation. Helicopters and light aircraft had been spotted buzzing over his crop; he was convinced that police had him under surveillance. Sure, it was our handiwork, but it was just a random thing. Flights go over that region of Victoria quite regularly. It was nothing out of the ordinary.

He was also worried about an incident with his crop from a few nights before. Someone was after his dope and, unless an alibi was coughed up, he had everyone in his sights. Being the new boy on the block, Hancock suspected me as well. I knew a lot of the details of his dope-growing operation, so to him I was a perfect fit.

Although the idea was ridiculous, we had to divert

suspicion, so one of the Bairnsdale coppers told him that a Traralgon bloke, an enemy of Hancock's, was seen in town that night. I also put out the word that I was in Tasmania on the night of the crop raid. It seemed to do the trick, but there was still a noticeable change in Hancock's mood towards me.

'I tell you, John is a fucken joke,' I complained to both Hancock and Strong. 'Next year we'll fucken know better than to take somebody's word. But now, this year, we've got to keep ourselves out of the shit. We've promised a lot of people a lot of different things.'

'I know your position 'cause I've done it before too,' said Strong.

'And it's not just like embarrassment, it's fucken dangerous, you know.' No one seemed to give two shits about my apparent conundrum, so I changed tack. 'Okay, what's the tops you can get us then?'

'Say, eighty, and then the rest a month later,' said Hancock.

'So in a month's time we'll have two hundred?'

'Yeah, but in two lots.' Strong was ramming this part of the deal home, but I wasn't giving up without a fight.

'See, basically we want to get as much as we can in one scoop, and keep out of the fucken trouble. We don't want to sort of give people dribs and drabs.'

Although calm, Strong was beginning to lose patience with me. 'Well, do it elsewhere. You can do it elsewhere. I mean, I can fucken do it elsewhere.' Strong then walked off to take a slash, giving me an opportunity to work on Hancock.

'Listen, Bill, I understand where Graham's coming from, but we can't do it in two lots. We're fucken losing a lot of blokes who are putting in cash for this.'

Damian Marrett

Hancock finished off his pot of Carlton and ordered another round. I wasn't even sure if he was listening to me. 'Yeah, well, that's how he wants it, Damian,' he finally said, handing me a fresh one.

'What I want is, say in four weeks, just grab what you've got and then I'll give you the cash,' I said.

'If you can tell us what you want next year...'

'Mate, you know we'll always take everything you can get us, but it's dependent on this year,' I said. 'We've gone from blokes who can do, like, a thousand to a couple of losers scraping around for eighty or two hundred, you know.'

Strong returned from the gents', and I then spent the next hour intermittently trying to supersize the deal into one. It was difficult to keep things on track when all Brian wanted to do was talk to Strong about his bodybuilding regimen. The abs, the pecs, the deltoids and the 'roids, it was all too much. I was immediately transported back to the office, and the horrors of transcription.

If that wasn't enough, Hancock was just as disinterested. He wanted to talk about his intruder the other night.

'I was in here last night, and a fella came up and he said, "What were ya doin' takin' potshots the other night?"' Hancock said.

I laughed. Gary Aldridge had told me on the phone that Hancock had fired off a few rounds. Obviously word had spread. 'Fair dinkum. I thought it was a joke at first when Gary told me. I was down in Tassie, and all this shit was going on. Fucking unbelievable.'

Anyway, for the next hour I did my best to talk up the deal, but all we could agree upon was 200 pounds in two separate lots, 80 pounds the first. Cost: three and a half thousand per pound. The first deal was set for a fortnight's time. The second deal? Well, that one would have to be put permanently on hold after we busted these blokes.

Fast forward a couple of weeks, and Brian and I were back at Marshall's Hotel for a spot of lunch with Bill Hancock on March 29th. Although Melbourne was experiencing a dry spell, Gippsland was wetter than a sponge in the ocean.

'I had to bloody throw away five pound this morning,' said a narky Hancock. 'Mould gone through the head. It's not worth bloody messing around with.'

'Yeah? So, have we got anything for tomorrow?'

'Tomorrow? Oh, I've got fifteen pound there now, and I hope to have another fifteen dry today. I just picked another four this morning,' he replied.

'Thirty-four? That's all?'

'I'll try and see what I can get off John as well,' he said. 'But the hardest part at the moment is getting the stuff dry.'

'I've got a hairdryer in the car,' I wisecracked — a poor attempt, to be honest.

'No, well, I only started drying it yesterday, see. I put it in the sun for four hours,' he said, ignoring my smartarse comment.

'If it's close, you know, even if it's still wet, we'll take it. We just want to get as much as we can straightaway. We can lay it out in Thommo's shed,' I lied. Brian nodded absently. I didn't know Thommo personally (his name just appeared in my head), but by all accounts he had a dirty great big shed, ideal for drying out wet cannabis.

'I've also got a crop out the other way,' said Hancock. 'It's the best of the lot. Two weeks of fine weather, and I reckon there'd be a hundred and fifty pound there.'

'Fucken great. When the other one's ready I'll get you to find out who's looking at who, but we'll come back for that, no worries,' I said, knowing Hancock was convinced that he was under surveillance.

'It's just the coppers, that's all,' he said. 'I got some info that the flying squad's up here next week.'

'Who's the info from?'

Hancock looked briefly into his glass of lemon squash before taking a mouthful. 'Can't say, but it's someone who knows.'

I knew exactly who it was: on our instruction, a Bairnsdale cop was feeding him disinformation. We wanted to pressure Hancock so that the deal was done with us as soon as possible.

'Yeah, well, we should be right for this week. I won't come back for a couple of weeks, you know, be careful,' I said. 'We even hired a car for this visit. Got a mate who does it. No documents, no trace.'

I slipped that one in because it was important that Hancock knew we were also taking precautions. All of this surveillance had taken a toll on his judgment, and I didn't want him to think that he was attracting any increased police presence because of me.

'No worries then, mate. Give us a call tonight and we'll work out the details. I reckon early tomorrow's the go. No traffic, round about dawn.'

'It'll just be the two of us,' I said, looking over at Brian. 'You'll be by yourself, right?'

'Yeah, just me,' he said, throwing down the last of his drink.

'Alrighty,' I said. 'I'm just gonna finish up this beer, so I'll call you tonight.'

Hancock then exited the pub. Ten minutes later, Brian and I did the same. On the way out I noticed Hancock and his son Jarrod sitting tight in a yellow Commodore up the

Undercover

main street. They were obviously keeping watch to see if we were being watched. We jumped in the car and took off, hopefully allaying their fears.

After lazing around for a few hours, I placed a phone call to Hancock at 8 p.m. The deal was confirmed: Hancock had fifty pounds of cannabis for us, fourteen of the deal courtesy of John Dugdale. He told us that the transaction would be conducted in two parts, the first with him at six-thirty in the morning, the second with Dugdale a few hours later.

With everything set to go for buy/bust, about twenty Drug Squad officers joined us at a motel in Metung. Although the crew contained only two or three SOG boys, another twenty local coppers were prepared to provide back-up. We weren't short on manpower.

'The time is now 6:27 a.m. My name is Damian Marrett. I'm a Detective Senior Constable currently attached to the Victoria Police Drug Squad. Today is Tuesday the 30th of March, 1993. I'm performing duties in relation to Operation Twin in the Orbost area. I've just telephoned the target, William Hancock. I told him that I'd meet him at the Murrangowa truck stop, where we'd exchange $175 000 cash for fifty pounds of cannabis.

'Hancock will provide thirty-six pounds of cannabis initially; the other fourteen pounds of cannabis will be provided by the Dugdales, a family of targets up the road at Club Terrace. That deal will be completed later in the day.'

Ten minutes later, the tape was recommenced when Hancock arrived at the truck stop, his mode of transport a Honda Prelude coupé. After he opened the boot of his vehicle, I made my way over. Inside the boot and back seat, the car was chockers with boxes and bags spilling over with grass.

'Jesus, Bill, you could do with a station wagon,' I joked. 'I've gotta give you what, a hundred and twenty-six, right?'

'Right, yeah. I didn't even work it out. Yeah, the other fourteen's separate, but this isn't all of it. The boys have got another ten.'

'Your boys?' He was talking about his two sons, Jarrod and Darren.

'Yeah, they're a few minutes away.'

'Shit, more? Okay, we'll start moving it over.'

As we packed up our hire car, a white Commodore, Hancock explained the nitty-gritty of the dope's properties. What was wet, what was dry, the weights, even the weight of the boxes. Very thorough, was our Billy.

Just when I thought he was going to talk about the ratio of seeds to head, a yellow Commodore cruised into the truck stop, the same yellow Commodore we spotted yesterday outside Marshall's Hotel. Jarrod and Darren had arrived.

We filed over to the car, and the boot was flipped. Inside were a further half-dozen garbage bags full of cannabis. Everything seemed to be in order, so I walked back over to our car with a bag at a time. Bust time. Bust signal.

'Pleasure doing business with you, Bill,' I said with a smile. That was the signal.

Seconds later, blokes burst out of bushes, slapping the cuffs on the Hancocks before they even knew what was happening. With the deal conducted out in the open, we had no fear of others watching us, so this time I was a free man. There were smiles all round on our side of the law. It was a textbook buy/bust — targets arrested, drugs seized.

At first Hancock was dirty on me, but the wind had been taken out of him. He didn't verbal me, but he had a look on his face that showed where his head was at. He hated my guts. We'd really put one over him.

'You're in the shit, Bill,' I said. 'You might like to think about cooperating.'

Hancock was defeated, but he wasn't stupid. 'What do you want me to do?'

'Well, the Dugdales are next. Give us a hand, and we'll help you out. No promises though.'

'Yeah, but what do you want me to do?'

'Just give Dugdale a call. Tell him that the deal's on, nothing to worry about, business as usual.'

If Hancock didn't get on board, he knew that it could be a year or two tacked onto his sentence. It was a no-brainer. Under our supervision, he called John Dugdale to confirm the deal would go ahead.

Unable to drive back into Orbost for fear of alerting Dugdale that Hancock was in custody, we had a three-hour wait on our hands. In the interim Hancock was set another task. We wanted him to remain a presence during the Dugdale component of the buy/bust. A fellow dope grower's presence at the deal would lend an air of authenticity to the proceedings, we believed. Dugdale was a naturally cagey crook, and Hancock's attendance could act as a calming influence.

'Today is the 30th day of March, 1993, a Tuesday. This is Senior Detective Damian Marrett attached to the Victoria Police Drug Squad. I'm performing duties in relation to Operation Twin. The time is now 11 a.m. I'm with target Bill Hancock at the Murrangowa truck stop, where it's envisaged that target John Dugdale will arrive soon and a transaction will take place — a buy/bust situation for fourteen pounds of cannabis. I'll stop the tape here and recommence it on Dugdale's arrival at the truck stop.'

'Tape recommenced at 11:15 a.m. Dugdale has just pulled into the truck site.'

A gold Holden station wagon pulled up alongside the two of us. Inside was John Dugdale.

'G'day John,' I said.

'How's this fucken weather, hey?' Hancock said.

'Yeah I know,' said Dugdale. 'Fuck, I had this gear here fucken dryin' out for about three days, and yesterday the fucken rain, then the fucken sun. I didn't know what to do. Cover it up, fucken let it out ...' Sounded like a typical Melbourne day to me.

Dugdale then removed two very large black garbage bags full of dope from his boot, and sat it in front of us. 'Throw it in Bill's car,' I said. 'I'll go fix the money. It's in my car. Two secs.'

I then walked over by myself and opened the boot. This was our bust signal. There wasn't even any cash in the boot, so I stood nervously like a bunny in the spotlight waiting for the bust. And waiting. No response.

'For fuck's sake,' I whispered, 'the boot's fucking open. Do it. Fucken do it.'

Still, nothing. Rooted to the ground, now I felt like a bunny in the spotlight with a target on its back. After a minute or so I had no choice but to return to the others, and I had bugger all to work with. This was becoming something of a regular occurrence. What the fuck was I going to say? Hopefully all those training exercises would kick in through osmosis.

'Where's the money?' asked Dugdale upon my return. It wasn't the most unreasonable of requests.

'Yeah, well, funny about that,' I said. 'I, um, I haven't got any.'

'Stop playing funny buggers,' he snarled. 'We're doin' a deal. Get the fucken money.'

'I'm pretty sure Brian's got it,' I said at the last minute.

Undercover

'You know Brian, the Irish bloke? I think he's taken that other bag. He's back in five.'

'You think he has? I hope you're fucken joking,' Dugdale scowled.

I walked back over to the car, this time Dugdale right on my arse. Once again I flipped the boot, another clear signal to the bust crew that I was well and truly ready for their intervention. 'See,' I said, rummaging around, 'it's not here. Brian's got it. He'll be here any second.'

'Why did ya go and do that?'

'It's fine, it's just . . .'

Finally, the bust swung into gear. Cops swooped on the lot of us from behind anything that provided cover. Dugdale's legs collapsed underneath him as two local cops jumped on his shoulders and head.

After being handcuffed, John Dugdale was dragged to his feet. He appeared almost paralysed, glued to the ground, his facial expression on pause. He'd been completely stooged.

The hard man in the Gippsland growing community then puffed his chest out, a knowing half-smile finally revealing itself. You could just tell he was already preparing himself for the next chapter in his life. This was a sweet victory for the good guys. I hated the bloke.

Moments later, I asked one of the surveillance team about the delay. The bust signal didn't get through because the bloke who had the eyeball to give the word was also in possession of a dodgy radio. He was frantically signalling, but no one could hear him.

It sounds ridiculous now, but problems like this one were all too common in police surveillance circles. The radios were always tuned, but they could still drop their code for whatever reasons. It was usually something in the area we couldn't control, and communications always was, and still is, one of covert policing's biggest problems. The best squads in the world have the same difficulties.

Once Dugdale and the Hancocks were under lock and key, we started raiding everyone with a connection. Hancock's house was already being torn apart, so now it was time to turn our attention to Graham Strong and the other Dugdales. Some went quietly, others not so. Steven Dugdale, brother of John, was maced in the face during a violent confrontation. In the scuffle, one of his eyes was gouged pretty severely.

The next day we shifted our focus to Lakes Entrance. Anyone who dealt us drugs in the town was in our sights. When the Club Hotel was raided, a drug-dealing bikie in a wheelchair was mouthing off at a group of coppers. This bloke was known around town as deadset prick.

'Leave us alone, ya copper cunts!' he screamed.

He then tried to make a getaway on two wheels, his arms windmilling beside him. When they caught up to him, he got even more lippy.

'I'm in a fucken wheelchair, ya cunt. What are you gonna do?' he spat at one of our officers, once again trying to wheel his way to freedom.

One of them picked a stick up off the ground, slamming it into the wheelchair's spokes. The chair buckled, and the bikie's body was flung into the air. He landed chest-first onto the gravel.

'Pick us up, ya fucken arsehole!' he cried, attitude still intact.

'Safer if you stay there, pal,' said one of the detectives, turning his attention to any other bikie proving to be a handful.

'Just pick me up, ya gutless fucken pig.'

Undercover

'Shut up, will ya, pal, it's not Year of the Disabled. Well, not today anyway.'

Raids on these bikies netted large amounts of cannabis and powders, and the job was considered a huge success.

Back in Melbourne, there was just the one more miscreant to take care of: our double-crossing informer Gary Aldridge. I was still trying to organise the ten-pound deal of amphetamines, but he was stalling. It appeared that the amount was out of his league, and the deal was fizzing out, much to everyone's disappointment.

The next night, Bull called him up to arrange an employer–informer meeting at the New Orleans Hotel in South Yarra. Aldridge still didn't know I was a cop, and he certainly didn't know I was a colleague of Bull Pitt's. So I thought I might rock up unannounced at the pub for a parma and a pot.

When I waltzed into the bistro, Gary and Jim were settled in at a quiet table out the back.

'Gary, what are you doing here?' I said, doing a double take.

He looked over towards me, momentarily in a blind panic. Still, he pulled himself together quickly enough. 'G'day Damian. This is a mate of mine from Cann River,' he said, gesturing towards Bull.

I squinted my eyes at Bull, advancing for a closer look. 'Nah, nah, not him. He's a fucken pig! I've seen him before. He's a fucken drug cop!'

'Nah, nah, nah, mate, this is Bull, a friend from the country,' he said, his face turning to shit.

'I see what's going on. I fucken knew it! You're setting me up. You fuckers!' I raged, at the same time reaching for a gun inside my backpack.

I took a step back, and motioned as if I was pulling it out. My actions were obvious to Gary: I was going for my gun. He bellowed like some flaky Hollywood action hero. 'Nooooo!'

Before I could get the gun out, Gary jumped all over me and the backpack, bringing both of us to the ground. Bull calmly walked over and slapped the handcuffs on Gary Aldridge's wrists. Twin had run its course.

Postscript

The morning after John Dugdale's arrest, we travelled back to the site of the alleged crop out past Club Terrace. It was daylight, but we couldn't locate anything. There were, however, large crops discovered in the days after — just not in that location.

After Aldridge's arrest, I asked him why he was so spooked the night we visited the crop. He wouldn't answer. I then asked him if the crop existed in the first place. He wouldn't answer. Having said all that, Aldridge was a bit scared of me at the end.

The night of Gary Aldridge's arrest, he was stabbed at the Melbourne Remand Centre.

GOING DOWN

List of Principal Charges and Sentences

John DUGDALE
- 4 charges of trafficking a drug of dependence
- 2 charges of possessing a drug of dependence

Sentence: 2 years

Damian Marrett

Bill HANCOCK
- 4 charges of trafficking a drug of dependence
- 1 charge of conspiracy to traffic a drug of dependence
- 2 charges of possessing a drug of dependence

Sentence: 18 months

Graham STRONG
- 1 charge of conspiracy to traffic a drug of dependence
- 1 charge of trafficking a drug of dependence

Sentence: 9 months

Gary ALDRIDGE
- 2 charges of trafficking a drug of dependence (amphetamine)
- 1 charge of conspiracy to traffic a drug of dependence (amphetamine)

Sentence: 2 and a half years

Nine

July 1993–January 1994

There is no typical starting point to an undercover operation. However, a job is usually kicked off by one of two things: police intelligence or a willing informer.

Military intelligence might be an oxymoron but, from my experience, police intelligence isn't. We worked off it all the time. An example might play out this way: local police in Richmond are concerned that heroin use is on the increase. On the street, it's noticeable that a lot of people are high, junkies are overdosing more frequently, foils and syringes are being left discarded in gutters, and increased traffic has been observed going into certain houses.

After being fully briefed on the situation, we'd go down and check it out for ourselves. Sometimes we'd get lucky, and instead of nabbing just the dealers, we'd expose and arrest the suppliers as well.

Other operations may have involved an informer at their core. Most crooks understandably wanted a bit of leniency when we busted them, but you don't get something for nothing. We expected information on known associates before striking a deal. Hopefully the next step would be a direct introduction from the crook-turned-informer.

Another type of informer was a rarer breed: not ostensibly driven by the threat of prosecution, he would willingly give up information, usually without us having to exercise our influence. More like a part-time copper in the criminal world, he would get off on the buzz, the secrecy, the intrigue of informing.

These blokes were often considered dangerous, and before we put them on our books, we had to consider their motivations for informing. Some of them were just shitbag crooks. Coppers would toss them $20 for a cab or $100 of phone credit to encourage them. But the danger was that sometimes they believed that the exchanged information entitled them to some 'credits' in the future — a bit of a green light.

Gauging an informer's motivations was a crucial process. Many couldn't be trusted. Some criminals would inform only to suit themselves, turning to the police when they wanted to eliminate competition. They would dob in their direct drug-dealing rival to the cops and wait for their business to boom.

Thankfully, others were genuine in their approach. If an informer was willing to give up good criminals, thousands of dollars could feasibly change hands and relocation was provided. Even so, many were under the misapprehension that, once they started their new life, they'd be swimming in money (and still be allowed to go round to Mum's for a Sunday roast). Others thought they'd be set up in a New York penthouse. I can guarantee that's not where Australia's protected witnesses and informers end up.

The ones who came to us were pretty rare, however. A more regular occurrence involved working away on one group of criminals, enjoying success and locking some of them up. Weeks, sometimes months, later someone on the periphery of that group would call me up, unaware that I was a policeman. He was now filling the drug-dealing hole left by his mates in jail. Would I be interested in continuing to deal? Don't see why not. Count me in.

Having said all of that, the biggest undercover operation of my career simply landed in my lap.

Operation Afghan commenced as a joint initiative between the National Crime Authority (NCA) and the Rover Taskforce (an arm of the Victoria Police Drug Squad). The NCA had originally posed two questions after the Cerberus Taskforce conducted an investigation into organised crime. One: is there a Mafia presence in Australia? And two: if so, to what extent is it involved in organised crime?

The Rover Taskforce listed five main Victorian targets for the investigation. One of those targets was Pat Agresta, a connected wheeler-and-dealer known to police through past indiscretions and associations. Surveillance had picked him up enjoying a cuppa with several Lygon Street identities on the famous café strip.

When Agresta suddenly nicked off to Griffith one day, a bloke named Mark Gleeson from the Victoria Police Drug Squad surveillance team followed him.

'Crossing state lines' wasn't a concern for Gleeson. If it was an organised job the protocol was sometimes different, but Victoria Police would often follow crooks interstate, not even bothering to inform the local authority. I'm aware that it never panned out that way on *The Dukes of Hazzard*.

Anyway, you didn't have to be a super-sleuth to twig that Griffith was this country's epicentre of Mafia activity. All the big deals were hatched in the Riverina town. Italians of a particular persuasion were drawn to the joint like a gangster to Crown Casino.

After tailing Agresta one night to the Griffith Ex-Servicemen's Club, Mark had one eye on him while feeding coins into the pokies. The surveillance cop was with another of the Drug Squad crew, Alison. They knew that the Mafia boys would be drinking there, but they also knew that these blokes were hardened, tight criminals, uneasy in new and unfamiliar company. Mark's job was to observe them. Meeting and befriending them was pie-in-the-sky stuff.

It was then that Mark spotted a drunk woman who seemed to be friendly with the 'family'. She appeared to be in a shout with them, but was also trying her luck on the pokies at the same time. Her buddies were all heavy-duty crooks — members of two of the most prominent Griffith families, the Romeos and Trimbolis, were among them. Mark sensed an in. He figured he was in the right place at the right time.

Playing the machine next to her, he struck up a conversation. They hit it off, and he introduced the woman to his 'girlfriend', Alison. After an hour or so of friendly chitchat, she then introduced the two of them to her Mafia mates. The way she worded it, you'd have thought that she and Mark had known each other for years. It was all the encouragement the newly anointed undercover operative needed.

Alison was also making her presence felt to the crooks. It was well known in police circles that the Griffith lads considered themselves A-grade pantsmen. In the past few months, surveillance tapes had recorded a few of them enjoying the services of a well-known Melbourne brothel. Alison played up to this fact, at one stage sitting on Ross Trimboli's lap, paying him far more attention than he deserved. Although Alison was 'attached' to Mark, the local gangsters thought they were in, without even having to exchange cash.

It turned into a big night, drinking and eating into the early hours. When the night wound down at 4 a.m., a group of half a dozen stragglers were firm friends. Phone numbers were exchanged, and future plans were hatched in more ways than one.

Mark developed a cover story on the spot. For the purposes of the infiltration, art lover Mark became art dealer Mark. His business took him to Canberra, and he often drove through Griffith on his way home to Melbourne.

Thankfully, the ruse didn't require an inordinate amount of backstopping (the police practice of setting up the background and paperwork when an operative takes on a new identity). Almost immediately, a company was registered and backdated in Mark Gleeson's name, an apartment was maintained in East Melbourne for the happy couple, ID was secured, car registration was taken care of, chequebooks were printed, as were letterheads, business cards and flyers.

Over a period of months, relationships developed naturally. Mark and Alison would visit art galleries in Canberra on business. To break up the drive, they would drop in on their new mates in Griffith afterwards. Dinner and accommodation was always taken care of by the family. Before their return to Melbourne, the car would be loaded up with free crates of oranges and wine. Even when Alison took some leave and went to Darwin for a holiday, she placed Ross Trimboli on her postcard list.

When Ross and Tony Romeo conducted business down south, they made an effort to call in on Mark and Alison at the East Melbourne apartment. Evenings were spent dining free on Lygon Street. A lover of the good life, Mark was eating well with none of the expense. Food and drink on Carlton's premier eating strip was always on the house for Tony Romeo and Ross Trimboli, two of Australia's most respected Mafia men.

Mark was repaying them in kind. Ross had lost his New South Wales driver's licence, and required an interstate one to get back on the road — in those days the computers weren't nationally linked. For the purposes of obtaining a Victorian licence, Mark allowed Ross to use the East Melbourne premises as his address.

Mark also continued to push his art dealership, explaining to the Calabrians how easy it was to conceal money through purchasing artworks. He was then introduced to the organisation's accountant, who described in detail a number of tax avoidance scams that could be run through the dealership's books.

The accountant gave the undercover cop several tasks to complete. Mark opened false bank accounts and purchased expensive artworks. The acquisitions ran into hundreds and thousands of dollars. In a little under six months, Mark was well liked by the Italians. He was non-threatening, middle-class, refined; a regular at Christie's auctions, Mark Gleeson was too polished to be a copper. Without them questioning it, the policeman had become an integral member of the organisation.

One night, Mark and Alison hosted a dinner party at their apartment. The place was fitted out with the latest in audio and video surveillance technology, and Ross Trimboli was one of the guests. During the course of the meal, Mark mentioned that he had a friend who worked in the music industry. As a consequence, the phrase 'sex, drugs, and rock 'n' roll' came up in conversation. Ross then casually, yet quietly, explained to Mark that the 'drugs' component was easy to come by. Cocaine was a particular house specialty.

Once they started talking drugs, Alison was moved into the background. Not only was she an untrained operative, but a job of this magnitude required someone with different chromosomal make-up — Italians never involve females in criminal activities. Mark and Alison were still an 'item', but the bosses decided another male presence was needed to keep the operation running on track. Enter 'brother' Ben.

Mark first approached me in December 1993 at an undercover course I was lecturing in. How the worm had turned. Nearly two years ago they were threatening to throw me off the course; now they wanted me to chip in and help with training. Oh, the irony of it all ...

I knew Mark from the Drug Squad, but we'd never worked closely on a job before. His main concern was trust. He was already deep undercover, and he didn't want someone coming into the job now and ruining all his hard work. I'd gained something of a reputation by that stage, having had some success on a range of jobs. He was keen to sound me out.

Mark explained in great detail the background to the sting. It certainly was a job of mind-blowing proportions. 'Two deals are on the table already,' he said. 'One's a small cannabis deal, twelve pounds. The other's a big one, a kilo of coke.'

'When are they due to be done?' I asked.

'As soon as they can get the gear. Could be as early as next week.'

'Great, get right into it,' I said, itching to jump on board the Afghan express.

'They mentioned that you're in between jobs,' he said.

'I've got a couple of things, but mate, I'd love to do it. It's got everything.'

'So you're in?'

'Say hello to your new brother.'

We shook hands; Mark and I were now family. On reflection, we probably didn't look like brothers. Mark was fairer skinned and had a few more pounds around his girth. He was also more than ten years older, but we knew that the crooks had already made a decision to trust everything about Mark. They had no reason to doubt his word that his little brother was his little brother. Or half-brother, as the case was. Just to clear up any confusion about our looks, we decided from the start that our mothers were unrelated.

It made sense: compared to his brother Ben, Mark was a different beast altogether.

When not working undercover (and even when he was), Mark Gleeson's background shaped him in some respects. In his early forties, and a ten-year veteran of the Drug Squad, he'd grown up in Richmond before the inner-city suburb had been gentrified to within an inch of its life. As a kid he'd done it tough, often going without the basics. No surprises then that he had this thing about money.

A smart dresser topped off with a well-groomed handlebar moustache, Mark was something of an expert on wine, food, and art. The ideal person to dazzle targets like the Griffith Mafia, he simply loved the finer things in life.

By his own admission, Mark had stumbled by chance into what eventually became Operation Afghan. Although not overly experienced in undercover work, he landed on his feet with a score of ten from the Russian judges.

My undercover image couldn't have been any more contrary. I was street smart, a larrikin with long hair worn lazily in a ponytail. I was a T-shirt and jeans sort of guy. Mark wouldn't even paint his house in some of the clothes I wore out on the town.

From that first meeting we both knew we had to work extensively on our cover stories. It was determined that I

Undercover

was Mark's younger half-brother with a bit of dash about him. Cocaine might have been Ross Trimboli's house specialty, but the knockabout larrikin was mine. In my spare time I was a house renovator, buying houses cheaply, doing them up, and selling them on. When I wasn't polishing floorboards I was buying drugs cheaply, dividing them up, and selling them on. The money I made through drugs was laundered through the renovating business.

In little more than a week, we were ready. Our covers sounded perfectly legit, and I felt that Afghan couldn't have come at a better time. I was really enjoying my work, only recently handpicked as one of eight operatives in a newly formed professional undercover unit. Four were chosen from the Victoria Police Drug Squad, with the other four coming from the Bureau of Criminal Intelligence (BCI).

We said goodbye to the grimy confines of Russell Street, moving into our own specially designed office space renovated from the guts of a large warehouse in Melbourne's inner suburbs. The location was, and still is, a closely guarded secret.

There were no interruptions then, no bullshit. You were treated as elite. I was even assigned a special agent number. From then on, I was covert operative number 003. That's double-oh-three, Marrett, Damian Marrett. Tragically, 007 had already been snapped up by another undercover.

As with anything new, there was a lot of money thrown at us. The bosses were very eager for it to work. So we felt like we had the money, the structure and the professionalism to pull off the big jobs.

The only problem was the two conflicting cultures. Drug Squad coppers were known to fly by the seat of their pants on an operation. This approach was sometimes reckless, possibly dangerous, but often we'd come up with results because of it.

To us, BCI were like robots. They'd check their fucking rubbish, check the crooks' fucking rubbish, draw a flowchart, analyse the flowchart, and then draw another one with very minor alterations. After lunch they'd talk through the job, detailing all the information a flowchart was unable to provide them. That information would then be incorporated into a super flowchart that covered two whiteboards, the second one acquisitioned at the last minute from Russell Street, delivery time two days. Then, and only then, would they go into a job.

In the time it took the BCI crew to do all that, we were three beers into a shout at the local, the crooks safely tucked away under lock and key. Well, that's how I saw it anyway.

Understandably, there was friction between the two camps. The work environment was always split between us. We still drank together, but we had different ways of doing things. We'd bag them behind their backs, as they did us. To give you an idea: my copy of an operation's file would be coffee-stained only on the front page. Theirs would be coffee-stained, notated and dog-eared on every page. In short, the BCI boys were big on theory. We were big on practice. Or ... they were thorough, and I was a lazy bugger.

Agent 003's first contact with Mark's Mafia mates came about when a twelve-pound deal of cannabis was being discussed. Mark was also making inroads into a one-kilo deal of cocaine.

When the first meeting was being organised for the East Melbourne flat, a little friction between Mark and I was already surfacing. While Mark was totally focused on

Afghan, I had other small jobs running at the same time. When he discovered I'd be posing as a hitman the morning of the first meeting, he was furious. I couldn't do anything about it though, so afterwards I raced around to the apartment as Ben Gleeson to meet Ross Trimboli for the very first time.

I came fully briefed about what to expect. Rosario 'Ross' Trimboli was already considered one of Operation Afghan's primary targets. A drug dealer by trade, and a money launderer by necessity, Ross's criminal bloodlines were impeccable: he was a nephew of dead Griffith godfather Robert 'Aussie Bob' Trimboli.

Thirty-five-year-old Ross ran with a ragtag collection of gangsters from Griffith in southern New South Wales with strong links to a ragtag collection of gangsters from Calabria in southern Italy. The media liked to call these crooks the 'Honoured Society' or the 'Black Hand'. In their quieter moments, they referred to themselves only as 'family'.

And most of them *were* family. Not only did they prefer to keep their business strictly in-house, these blokes didn't spread their swimmers too far from home either. Sure, most of them rooted around on their wives — but family was family.

So when I lobbed on Mark's doorstep, I felt like I was up to speed. Moments later I was in the living room, Mark playing host. 'Ross, meet my brother, Ben. Ben, this is Ross, and this is Roy.'

I shook Ross Trimboli's hand. 'Brother Ben, brother Ben, pleased to meet you,' Ross said cheerfully. It wouldn't be the last time someone called me 'brother Ben' from thereon in. 'This is my cousin Roy, Roy Romeo.'

Roy Romeo was Tony's brother. Even though his name was Rocco, people called him Roy because Tony Romeo had a cousin also called Rocco. Everyone called that Rocco 'Fifi' though. So I have no idea why neither of the two Roccos went by the name Rocco. All I knew was that Fifi didn't look like a Fifi. I didn't really care, because I enjoyed calling him Fifi. It was like everyone had a licence to take the piss out of him.

It was obvious from the outset that Ross was the bloke we'd be conducting business with. He talked a lot, and he talked fast. All torso, very little legs, he was a cross between Joe Pesci and Danny De Vito. Even so, like most Aussie Mafia men, his size didn't affect his standing in the organisation.

Business associate Roy was a different breed of cat. Although he appeared to be very polite every time I met him, I can't recall Roy ever uttering a word. He was a top-notch nodder though, his head always bobbing up and down for no reason. I wasn't sure if he was a simpleton or just shy.

'Now, there's a problem with the white,' said Ross.

'What's the problem?' I asked.

'We've been fucked around by our supplier,' he said. 'You know, we feel terrible about it.'

'That's no good at all,' I said. 'Our man wanted a sealed kilo tonight. If you can't get all of it tonight, he doesn't want any of it.'

'Mark mentioned that it's your own money, though,' said Ross.

'Yeah, I've got some money, but not enough for a kilo,' I said.

Mark took this as his cue, and he picked up a blue adidas bag from behind the couch. He opened it and showed Ross the money inside, maybe about $20 000. It was just bluff money to force their hand. The kilo was probably not coming, and hopefully we could do a smaller amount. You can also guarantee that the minute a crook sees money, things get done. The trick was to never lock yourself into anything. Keep all the options open.

Sure enough, after taking a look at the cash Ross was in dealing mode again.

'Hang in there, and I will show you that I can do it,' Ross said. 'This supplier, he's a fucken Turk. You cannot trust them. They'll put a cup of coffee in front of you and then they'll stab you in the back.'

'And then they'll make you pay for the coffee as well,' I joked.

The gag went down a treat; Ross pissed himself at the thought. 'You know, I'm fucked off too,' he said. 'It costs me two grand in expenses every time I come down to Melbourne.'

Bloody expensive hookers, I thought. 'What about the grass? Mark mentioned some green as well.'

'That I can help you with. You know, I understand grass more than white. I know the grass is good, but I'm not an expert on the white. I can't tell you whether it's good or bad. I have to trust others.'

'How much have you got?'

'Twelve.'

'Pounds or kilos?'

'Pounds. It's skunk, very good, and it'll be continuous from February. Fifty, one hundred, two hundred, whatever you want. We can even keep it in a house down here. You take some, sell it, and pay us in three to four weeks.'

Mighty trusting of him. It was plain to see that Mark was already very tight with Ross's organisation. They'd convinced themselves that he wouldn't rip them off or set them up. And anyway, no one with half a brain would fuck over the Mafia.

'How much a pound?'

'Four each,' Ross replied. Forty-eight thousand dollars was about the going rate for twelve pounds of cannabis — the bosses could live with that.

'You know, Ben will be able to take the lot. Even two hundred's no worries. He's got a lot of friends in Tassie,' said Mark, pumping up my tyres.

'Tasmania?' asked Ross.

'Yeah, there's a huge shortage over there. Ben reckons he can get 750 an ounce,' Mark said. At that time, the going rate for an ounce of cannabis on the mainland was $300. There's sixteen ounces in a pound, and if I bought the twelve pounds of grass for $48 000, I could conceivably on-sell it in Tasmania for $144 000.

'Fucken hell!' cried Ross.

'Jesus, shut the fuck up, Mark. Now they'll head over there,' I laughed.

'No, Ben, this is your job, not mine,' Ross encouraged. 'You can't work with people you can't trust. Take my word for it, boys. If you don't make money with us, you never will.'

'Yeah, sounds good.'

'We have to trust each other. This business, you know, it's like a woman,' said Ross, preparing to launch into a homespun homily. 'Once a woman is a slut, she is always a slut. If someone fucks you up in business, they'll always fuck you up.'

'No worries, Ross. You can rely on us,' I said, stifling a snigger.

'You know, you could be a bloody cop for all I care, but as long as you don't fuck me, I couldn't give a shit,' Ross said, rather prophetically. In fact, he was just trying to emphasise the worst example of a human being he could think of. It could just as easily have been a nigger, an Abo — even a murdering Turk who makes you pay for a coffee.

'We're not into fucking people round, mate. I can guarantee that.'

'Now, Mark is coming to Griffith in a few weeks,' said Ross. 'You'll be coming with him, yes, brother Ben?'

'Sure.'

'We'll have something ready for you when you come.'

Ross Trimboli was true to his word. He had something ready all right. Scared the bloody shit out of me too.

Ten

February 24-25, 1994

When explorer John Oxley downed tools in the Griffith area in 1817 as the first white man, he described the region as being 'uninhabitable and useless to civilised man'. Over 100 years later, an extensive irrigation scheme coupled with Walter Burley Griffin's design capabilities made a mockery of Oxley's proclamation. Whether or not some of Griffith's residents were civilised was still open to debate.

I drove into Griffith for the first time on February 24, 1994. Burley Griffin's signature wide boulevards and sweeping roundabouts immediately reminded me of Canberra, his more celebrated turn. The median strips housed midget palm trees, squatting like Calabrian farmers on smoko. I felt like I was in the right place.

Mackay's Furniture is one of the first large retail outlets you encounter on your way into town from the south — a bricks-and-mortar reminder of Griffith's bloody past.

The former proprietor of the shop, anti-drugs campaigner Donald Mackay, went 'missing' from the Griffith Hotel car park back in 1977. It's no great underworld secret that our target Ross Trimboli's uncle, Aussie Bob Trimboli, orchestrated the hit.

To this day, Mackay's body has never been discovered. As a drug trafficker with principal connections to the Mr Asia heroin syndicate, I guess you could say Uncle Bob was simply protecting his own interests.

Undercover

A Griffith street had even been named after Donald Mackay, the town's most famous ex-resident. No such kudos for Bob Trimboli, the town's most infamous ex-resident. As far as I could tell, Trimboli Terrace didn't make it past local council.

This being my first visit to Griffith, Mark and I had to negotiate the six-hour car journey from Melbourne to get there. Time went quickly enough, although Mark's approach to road trips was already beginning to give me the shits.

All he wanted to do was talk about the job: what might happen, what shouldn't happen, what we'll say, what they'll say. He was trying to play out the job before acceptances. Sure, I didn't mind a bit of healthy preparation for the task ahead, but I also loved my down time. Every attempt to listen to some music on the radio (or football when the drive coincided with a weekend) was met with Mark's hand reaching for the off switch. I wanted to relax. He wanted to talk shop. His compromise was ten minutes of radio, then thirty minutes of the job. It was that regimented.

Mark paid particular attention to the hierarchical structure of the Mafia. That night we were set to have dinner with, among others, the number two man in Australia, Tony Romeo.

'Now you'll notice, Ben, that when we sit down at the restaurant everyone will have their designated seats,' said Mark, calling me by my Afghan name to get himself into character. 'Tony Romeo will sit at the head of the table, Ross will slot in beside him, then me, then maybe you.'

'Yeah, yeah.'

'It's fascinating how it's all played out. You'll see what I mean when we get there. Now Tony's the main man, so we've got to work on him. We must respect the pecking order.'

'Okay, bro,' I said, looking at my watch. Twenty-six minutes until my next injection of radio.

'And for Christ's sake, don't be a smartarse. Not everyone understands your humour, you know.'

'But won't they learn to love it?'

'That's exactly what I mean. Just don't be a smartarse.'

Our accommodation was the Astra Motel on Griffith's main drag, Banna Street. It was a rather standard motor inn, but the 'family' had some sort of connection to the joint, meaning our bills were taken care of at checkout time. It was a great opportunity to give the minibar a decent nudge without it being some sort of guilty pleasure.

We were given the same twin room every time we hit town: 314. It was no Hilton, but it served our purposes. Melbourne people would be familiar with the design palette. Influenced heavily by an eighties Franco Cozzo catalogue, we're talking grey soft leather couches, dusty plastic plants perched on top of mirrored decorative pillars, and tastelessly carved wooden bed-heads above the two singles. Shouldn't whinge. Loved that free minibar.

The view from Room 314's balcony was one of the best in Griffith, looking southwards over the town. The scene to the east took in a light aircraft, a Navy issue Fairey Firefly suspended on a pole 15 metres in the air over one of Griffith's busiest intersections. A naval reconnaissance plane used in WWII and Korea, the Fairey Firefly had a red, blue and white target painted underneath each wing. I don't know, but if I was flying the thing, those two exposed bullseyes would give me the creeps.

With a Crownie in my hand I pointed the plane out to

our meet-and-greeter, Ross Trimboli. 'We'll definitely need a bigger one than that for New Guinea, hey Ross.'

'Yeah, Mark was talking about what plane was the best,' he said.

'I think he was saying a Piper or a Cessna would do the trick.'

'Okay.'

'He mentioned his mate the pilot, didn't he?' I asked.

'He can be trusted?'

'Yeah, I've met him a few times, but he's Mark's mate really. How's things your end?'

'Coming along fine. No worries, brother Ben.'

In late February the New Guinea deal was still in its infancy. It had all kicked off about a month earlier when Mark strategically mentioned that he had access to a pilot. Ross took his bait immediately, raising the possibility of importing a mountain of grass from our northern neighbours. He was confident that he could get his hands on a tonne (1000 kilograms or 2246 pounds) of the stuff.

At that time (and to this day), New Guinea was exporting tonnes of marijuana to Australia every year. The most popular mode of transportation between the two countries was by a vessel called a banana boat. Ostensibly a bloody big fibreglass dinghy, the banana boat came equipped with a powerful, souped-up outboard motor. They're the speediest 25-foot dinghies you're ever likely to see, probably twice as quick as your average speedboat.

The Australian Coastguard was well aware of the boat's capabilities; so much so that sales of the banana boat were banned on Cape York Peninsula in Far North Queensland.

Yet, in New Guinea, the banana boat was everywhere. New Guinean drug couriers would load up a boat at dusk in preparation for a return journey of no more than 300 kilometres. Great seafarers with amazing vision, the natives would navigate Torres Strait by the stars. When it was cloudy, they were so switched on to the water's ebb and flow that they'd use tidal discrepancies as their guide. Invariably they'd be back home by dawn with a fistful of cash or a cache of weapons for their troubles.

The Coastguard didn't lie down completely, though. On nightly helicopter jaunts they'd arm themselves with night-vision goggles in an attempt to track down these blokes. But the natives had an ace up their sleeves. The Torres Strait was considered their traditional fishing waters. When the Coastguard chopper buzzed them, they'd throw a line over the side of the boat, and wait. After an hour or so the helicopter would run out of juice. As soon as they took off to refuel, the banana boat would be on its way again, flat-knacker. It was real cat-and-mouse stuff.

For all of that, our plan was to chopper the cannabis from the New Guinea mainland to a secluded Australian airstrip on Horn Island (a tonne of grass would probably sink a banana boat). From Horn Island, our twin-engine Piper Navajo Chieftain seven-seater would pick up the gear and fly it down south for distribution.

Working out the logistics of the importation proved to be another thing, but at least we had a pilot already on board. In reality he was a Victoria Police Senior Sergeant plucked from the Melbourne Coroner's Court. We called him Jimmy. He had extensive light aircraft flying experience, and was enthusiastic about accepting the gig. He figured doing something he loved was better than pen-pushing.

After a little bit of research for our Griffith mates, we worked out that the Piper was capable of hauling a one-tonne cargo. The only problem was the landing in the

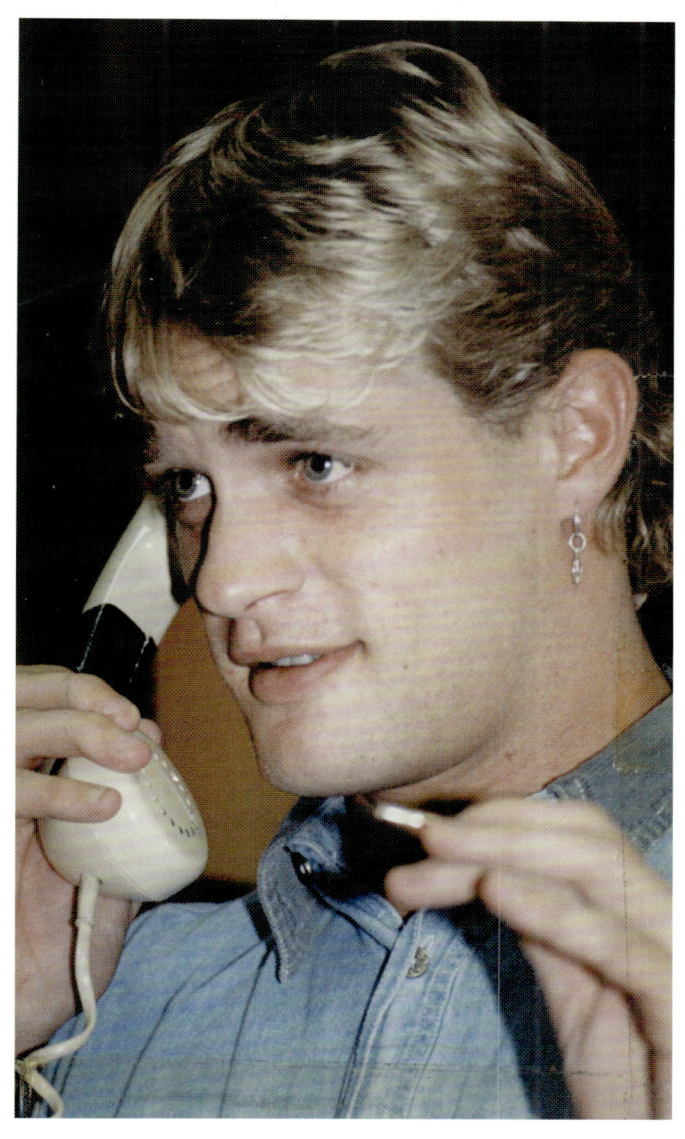

Office phones habitually took a beating.

All photographs from the collection of Damian Marrett.

Before   After

A pink-shirted Jim Ventrice and his toy poodle mullet agree to terms.

A bit of Bert in the morning. Big Patty Condro keen for a kip.

AM 8:49 18 JUN '92

The SOG pounce. I'm sprawled out next to the red 4WD, Patty Condro two cars to my left.

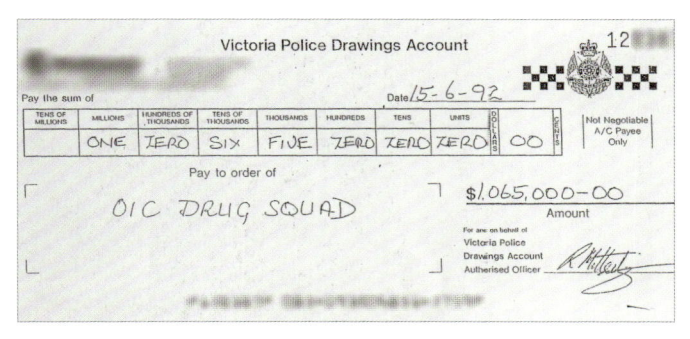

TENS OF MILLIONS	MILLIONS	HUNDREDS OF THOUSANDS	TENS OF THOUSANDS	THOUSANDS	HUNDREDS	TENS	UNITS	
	ONE	ZERO	SIX	FIVE	ZERO	ZERO	ZERO	00

Victoria Police Drawings Account

Date 15-6-92

Pay to order of OIC DRUG SQUAD

$1,065,000-00

For and on behalf of Victoria Police Drawings Account Authorised Officer

Approval for Operation Bert's buy/bust show money.

Down with Griffith.

The 'family' drop in for a cuppa. Domenic Trimboli (L) and Rocco 'Roy' Romeo at the East Melbourne apartment.

Smile for the camera. Rocco 'Roy' Romeo (L) and Ross Trimboli doing business.

Time out on the couch between drug deals in East Melbourne.

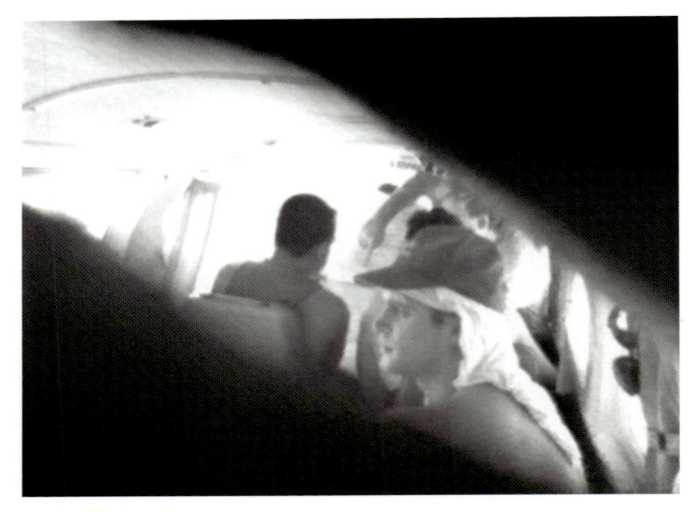

Surveillance photograph of dummy run to Horn Island, crap disguise on my head.

Phones as big as televisions — must be a lot of heroin in the bag.

$180 000 for the Afghan deal. The newspaper in the shot confirms the date.

Flanked by Tania and Rory — life after undercover at Fairfield CIB, Melbourne.

Highly commended for shiny shoes (and my work on Operation Afghan).

Undercover

Riverina: we needed something paved. There were concerns that if we brought the plane down on a dirt airstrip, the wheels would collapse underneath us. If we were lucky, the plane would bellyflop to a halt. If we were unlucky, the plane would burst into a fireball, one tonne of cannabis kindling providing the fuel.

To compound our dilemma, even some paved tarmacs couldn't sustain such a heavy load. We required an A1 airstrip, and finding a suitable sealed location close to Griffith became a top priority.

Ross was directing a lot of his energies into resolving all of the logistical risks and strategies involved in the importation, but he appeared to be on top of it all.

'Did I tell you?' he said, backed up against Room 314's balcony rail. 'We've had to change our plans on the helicopter.'

'How come?'

'Well, a regular chopper can't carry one tonne in weight. We're trying to get ourselves an army one, a bigger one.'

It probably never occurred to Ross to look at the problem from another angle. Something like reducing the load from a tonne to 500 kilos. Greed put paid to those ideas, if they ever surfaced.

'But one thing's still worrying me,' Ross continued. 'How does your man fly around without everyone knowing where he's going?'

'Don't worry about that,' I replied. 'Mark's got it all under control. He told me that, because we fly at 10 000 feet, nobody needs to know where we're going. We'll be staying away from the major cities, so radar won't pick us up at that altitude. Radar only picks you up when you're flying over 30 000 feet — you know, get the fuck away from our 747.'

'So you don't have to check in with anyone?'

'Nah, we can pretty much fly anywhere we want to. The only time we'll stop is to refuel. It's just like me driving up here to Griffith — I don't have to tell anyone where I'm going.'

'What about your mum?' Ross laughed.

'Especially not my mum,' I said.

Ross roared like an Italian man who was afraid of his mama.

We then made our way back into the motel room, where Mark was sprucing himself up after the long drive. By the time I threw on a fresh shirt, Mark was eager to make tracks to Benson's restaurant — and Tony Romeo.

Benson's was the Griffith gangster's first choice for fine dining. A cream brick eatery outside, it offered standard Italian fare inside. When I walked in with Ross and Mark, about four or five Calabrian gentlemen were waiting for us, already enjoying Benson's hospitality.

'Take a seat,' said Ross, pointing to a table set for ten. After Mark's little pep talk about hierarchical comings and goings, I plonked myself down next to Domenic Trimboli, Ross's brother. Introductions over, it appeared that our intended target, Tony Romeo, was fashionably late. Like most men in charge, he probably enjoyed testing out his colleagues' patience.

Thirty minutes later, Tony finally arrived. Well, I figured it had to be him. Of all the Griffith Italians, Tony was the only one with a modicum of style. He was the living embodiment of smart casual, dressed sharply in a pair of fashionable denim jeans and a pressed shirt. No matter the circumstance, Tony always carried himself well. He could've taught his business associates a thing or two about general deportment — Griffith Italians are notoriously sloppy dressers.

I got out of my chair when he approached the table. 'This is my brother Ben,' said Mark.

'Brother Ben, brother Ben, how are you going?' Tony asked, a welcoming and genuine smile coursing across his face.

'Thought you weren't coming,' I joked, playing that smartarse role Mark so feared.

Tony laughed instantly, putting his hand on my shoulder, and then taking a seat at the head of the table. 'Come up here, brother Ben, move up closer.' I edged two spots to my left, slotting myself next to Tony and directly facing Mark. So much for the strict dining out pecking order.

The rest of the night passed without incident. It was all just friendly shit, very enjoyable. The veal scaloppini was a treat. During the course of the evening, when I casually mentioned the New Guinea job, Tony admonished me. He was adamant that business was not to be conducted in such a setting or in front of certain ears.

'You boys, Mark, Ben, come back to my place afterwards,' he said. 'We'll have a nightcap, and we can talk.'

I was happy to do that. To tell you the truth, I was in and out of Benson's half the night exchanging batteries for my bloody mobile phone. It was one of those bricks favoured by tradesmen who were looking for a phone that was almost indestructible. We needed the battery to stay fresh because the phone also doubled as a transmitter. When we gave the word (usually by calling them up), our monitoring people dialled up the telephone, and it worked just as effectively as a listening device. Unlike the phone, the transmitter was the latest technology; but more on that shit of a phone later.

We left the restaurant at 10 p.m. to go to Tony's. In the hours beforehand, Ross had kept calling it 'the million dollar house'. When we pulled up outside I could see why, although sometimes when you throw money at something it doesn't quite stick; it kind of oozes down the walls like it would prefer to be somewhere else. Like maybe on something more tasteful.

'Welcome to my home, brother Ben,' said Tony, opening the front door.

'Thanks Tony. Love the house,' I said, glancing at the busy nature of the interior design. I counted at least half a dozen doors leading off to God knows where. It was a pretty swish affair. Six bedrooms, so Ross had told me earlier in the evening.

'Come through. What would you boys like to drink? Red wine okay?'

'Sounds good to me,' said a relaxed Mark, already familiar with his surroundings. He'd been to Tony's house on a number of occasions previously.

We walked through one of the doors, and into a distant room out the back of the house, used only for meetings. We made ourselves at home on the soft leather couches (Italians love that soft leather) while Tony fixed the drinks. A couple of Griffith reds placed on coasters in front of us, and we were down to business.

As always, Ross did most of the talking. The main issue of the day was the mechanics of the New Guinea importation. As mentioned earlier, we needed a convenient landing strip. Most of the airfields in the area were unpaved so it was likely we'd have to move further afield, possibly to northern Victoria.

While Ross fixed everyone a cognac, Mark and I spoke to Tony about our cut of the proceeds resulting from the deal. Just for organising the pilot, and assisting with the logistics, we were promised fifty kilos of the gear straight off the plane, with a chance to buy more at a vastly reduced rate down the track.

Tony did more listening than talking, the privilege of the man calling the shots. So it was difficult to work out what he was thinking, but he seemed happy with the deal's progress.

When Ross returned with another round of drinks, I placed a tentative finger on the mobile phone sitting next to me on the couch. Shit. It was happening again. The phone was cooking. This was the major problem with the phone. I could live with the hourly battery changes, but the fact that it had a nasty habit of overheating was another matter entirely. Before Afghan, I'd sent that bloody phone to the techs again and again. Every time it came back with the same problem.

Ross could see the phone was giving me grief. I probably gave the game away when I screamed out 'Fuck!' when I touched it. In fact, the mobile was so hot that when I lifted it up, the base of it momentarily stuck to Tony's leather couch, leaving a reminder (hopefully temporary) of its stay.

'What is it with that phone of yours?' Ross asked. 'I've gotta say, you know, it's way past its use-by date.'

'Yeah, yeah, I know. But it gets such great coverage,' I said, trying to divert suspicion. 'And it also doubles as an iron.'

'But there's something seriously wrong with it. Do yourself a favour. Get something smaller,' he said, picking it up and testing the weight. Little did he know that he was handling a listening device. Actually, handling's probably the wrong word — the phone was so hot that he was juggling it from palm to palm. 'This phone is a joke, right? Feel the weight on this, Tony.'

Damian Marrett

Tony Romeo perched regally in his chair, a cognac in one hand, waving Ross away with the other. He was totally uninterested in Ben Gleeson's big and boiling mobile phone. I was thankful: I didn't like one of our listening devices being handed from target to target like a game of pass-the-parcel. It just didn't sit well with me.

'Nah, look, when I work on houses, I'm dropping the thing all the time. With this one, no worries. Those new small ones break all the time.' This was my standard excuse for carrying around a piece of outmoded junk. It was handy having a renovating background.

'And you have to change batteries all the time,' said Ross. 'Look at you tonight — every five minutes you're putting in a new one.'

What was this, the fucking Spanish Inquisition? I never expected the Spanish Inquisition ...

'Thanks Ross, that reminds me — I'd better juice it up now,' I said, grabbing the phone/transmitter out of his hand.

'Who's gonna call you at this hour?' asked Ross, refusing to get off my case.

'I'm waiting on a girl,' I said, walking away with a smile on my face. That shut Ross up. I'd been told that he had a huge sexual appetite. He completely understood where I was coming from.

I then exited the room and house as casually as possible. It was important that the transmitter was up and running at a meeting like this one. You never knew when a conversation could take an interesting turn. The talk alone about the New Guinea deal was incriminating stuff.

And besides, I liked the idea of this transmitter-in-the-phone technology. It saved me all the stress of having to wear a wire. Mind you, I sometimes got a little buzz when a listening device was strapped on, especially when some

Undercover

great conversation was taking place. Wearing a wire was always a tempting mix of paranoia, panic and excitement. Just the sort of thing that made me love the job.

But I always had to be on my toes when I wore a wire. In the years preceding Afghan, I'd been patted down dozens of times. Sometimes I'd be searched when I least expected it, but I could usually sense when a target was about to pat me down. I'd be ready for it. One exception was the Asian drug dealers. No matter what the situation, they couldn't keep their hands off you. They were very polite about it though. Being forceful wasn't part of their nature.

But if I was worried that someone was about to check for a device, I'd back away and say something like, 'What are you doin' with my pager? Just leave it the fuck alone, you prick.' That would hopefully stop them in their tracks, and they'd usually forget what they were about to do in the first place.

I'd follow that up straightaway with a 'Who's that fucker over there? Is he with you? He looks familiar.' That usually muddied the waters enough. Once they'd missed that initial opportunity, it was often difficult for them to come back to it again.

At the risk of sounding like an old bloke at the bar dribbling into his beer, my day then was harder than it would be today. I had devices on me most of the time, and crooks were well aware that undercovers wore a wire. It's a different battleground now. The devices are so small, and located in places you wouldn't believe. The threat of detection is piddling.

When I returned from the car, where I'd changed the battery, the meeting was winding up. I thanked Tony for his hospitality, and he seemed happy that Mark's brother appeared to know his stuff — when he wasn't making excuses for his flaming mobile.

Damian Marrett

On the way to the front door, Ross bailed me up. 'Now, you like to party, yeah, brother Ben?'

'Whatever gave you that idea, Ross?' I said, the smartarse in me getting another airing.

'Just a guess,' he said, smiling. 'Well, next time you come up we'll have a big night, yeah?'

This wasn't the first time Ross had initiated this type of conversation. For months now he'd been into Mark about the possibility of a night out. For some reason the guy was very keen to party. It unsettled me. I had a feeling that Ross's definition of a big night out did not comply with my own. My ideal night involved a few drinks and a lot of laughs. Pretty standard stuff for a single bloke in his twenties. Ross was in his thirties, and I feared his idea of a party would involve sex and drugs, without the rock 'n' roll.

'Sounds good, mate. Count me in,' I replied.

'Yeah, sounds good,' added Mark.

'Leave it with me. I'll work out the details,' Ross said.

Details? Not much planning went into my drinking sessions. I had a feeling we'd set ourselves up for a night to remember.

The next morning Mark popped up to the shops, leaving me alone with Domenic Trimboli. He was about to shuttle us over to a local café for breakfast with his brother Ross. I needed a shower, so I turned the box on, telling Dom to get stuck into some Bert in the morning. Newton, that is. Not surveillance tapes of Patty Condro and his amazing talking nose.

A few minutes later I came out of the shower, earlier than expected, to look for my razor. At the same time Mark returned from the shops, only to discover Domenic Trimboli backing away from the bar fridge. He had a look on his face that said, 'I'm doing something I don't want you to know about.'

Mark had to challenge him. 'Are you right, Dom? What's going on?'

'Nothing mate, nothing. Just checking if you had enough beer in the fridge, that's all,' he said.

'Rightio. Cheers for that,' Mark said.

'I'll just finish off the job in the shower, chuck on some clothes, and then we'll get on the move,' I added.

'No problems,' Dom said to both of us, edging himself into the confines of soft leather.

I returned to the shower armed with a certain knowledge. You just couldn't beat the special brand of hospitality that the Astra Motel was providing us. They sent Domenic Trimboli into our room just to top up our fridge. Mighty generous of them.

I was sure the reality was something a little more sinister. Domenic was either planting a bug or disposing of a bug. Not trying to be too dramatic (or a wanker either), but the hunter had become the hunted.

This changed everything in an instant. Mark and I would now have to stay in character virtually all of the time. Although we were already doing that in case of this very situation, we would now have to be extra vigilant about it. I must admit, I'd had a few lapses in the past. Every now and then I'd say something and think to myself, 'Fuck, I hope they didn't hear that.' I was just hoping there wasn't already a device planted, or that they weren't listening to it all the time.

After I finished showering, we made our way out of the motel for a bite to eat. Before we left, I raced back to our Corolla. I had to pick up a replacement battery for the bloody useless mobile phone.

Damian Marrett

After opening up the car, I noticed straightaway that the glove box had been rifled through. Stuff that was previously in there was now on the floor. And they must've been in a hurry, because it was a sloppy job.

I wasn't sure if the car had been bugged, but I'd have to suss it out before we left Griffith in a couple of days. Just a routine check of all the obvious places should do the job — under the dash, the doors, under the centre console, under seats. I knew that they didn't have time to rip the car apart, and anyway, we had nothing to hide. Still, add that one to my growing list of concerns.

Come the afternoon, we had some time to ourselves in the motel room. I quietly got down on my hands and knees for a closer inspection behind the fridge. Nothing seemed out of place, but a day later our suspicions were confirmed when Special Projects Unit picked up some valuable information off the phone taps.

The crooks were making phone calls to each other, monitoring our movements. If we stepped out of the room for a bit of fresh air, a phone call was placed to Tony Romeo informing him of the fact. By all accounts he was getting constant updates, thanks to either the listening device planted somewhere in the room or his own surveillance. It was now official: we were following them following us following them!

That's when it started to freak me out a bit. They were playing the same game as us but from the other side, and it appeared they knew what they were doing. Now it was imperative that we had to be in our roles twenty-four hours a day. I have to say, Mark's concentration was far superior to mine in this regard, but from now on, no patented Damian Marrett fuck-ups would be tolerated.

Eleven

March 20, 1994

In roughly the time it takes to read this sentence, Ross Trimboli's 1991 red Porsche 911 Turbo had the capacity to accelerate from 0 to 100 kilometres per hour. To be precise, the car could do this in 4.9 seconds. I knew this because Ross repeatedly told me so.

Personally, I couldn't have given a shit about the performance capabilities of his Porsche. I'd never even ridden in one before. But Ben Gleeson was up for it. That car was his weakness.

And Ross clearly loved the car too. There was a running joke between the two of us that after we pulled off the big New Guinea job, it would be mine. I guess, in a strange way, the car *would* be mine. Well, ours anyway. The Drug Squad Asset Recovery Unit would be fighting over the scraps the minute Ross was in handcuffs.

Outside Griffith's Astra Motel, I let Ross catch me eyeing it off. 'You come in my car, brother Ben,' he instructed me.

I looked back at our hired blue shitbox, a Corolla hatchback. It suited Mark's cover story, but Ben Gleeson was definitely a red Porsche man. 'Yeah, I'll be in that,' I said to Ross, without a moment's thought.

Big mistake.

At this stage I was a month into Operation Afghan, still enjoying the buzz of undercover work. To all those around me, I was easygoing Damian. No job was too serious that I would let it get to me. But the nature and scope of this particular operation was beginning to unsettle me. For the first time in my life, the slightest prick of paranoia was threatening to affect my judgment. Two years of continual undercover work will do that to you.

Mark wasn't helping matters along either. He kept saying that we'd both be killed on this job or, more likely, in the months following it. I'm not sure if Mark truly believed that we would go the way of Griffith's favourite son, Donald Mackay, or whether he was just trying to get me to take the job more seriously. Either way, it was the last thing I wanted to hear in my state of mind.

On this particular day we were heading off to a barbecue at Tony Romeo's house. I wasn't wearing a wire, and I wasn't carrying a firearm. Although it was an honour to be invited, it was just a pissy little barbecue. We'd decided that a gun wasn't necessary.

But you wouldn't have known it by the stressed look on Mark's dial when I accepted Ross's offer of a ride in the Porsche. Was it because Mark was genuinely concerned for my safety — or was he pissed off that he was seemingly cut out of the action? Either way, I watched his face grow more and more uneasy in a matter of seconds.

And his uneasiness affected me too. It didn't worry me to the point that I would act or talk any differently, but there was just a nervy resonance in the back of my mind that something wasn't quite right.

I had my reasons. Ross Trimboli's behaviour the night before had been a bit erratic. Usually he was a warm, inviting guy who'd look you straight in the eye. Last night he was somewhere else. When I brought it up, he said somewhat cryptically that all would be explained later. He was in a better mood now, but clearly something was up.

In the days beforehand, we'd also received some potentially hazardous information. The Griffith 'family' was allegedly making regular payments of $100 000 each to a corrupt NSW politician, a tax officer and a senior NSW police officer. All three could potentially garner effective information about our undercover infiltration without so much as raising a sweat. When we saw Ross's behaviour the night before, Mark and I put two and two together, and thought, 'Shit, they might know we're cops.' I could just sense that something unexpected was about to happen.

Nothing we could do about it, so I hopped into Ross's car like a kid on cordial for the five-minute ride to Tony Romeo's brand-spanking new six-bedroom home.

'I'm bloody starving. Pig or cow?' I politely inquired. I was really looking forward to this Italian feast. I need regular meals. If I don't get them, I have a tendency to act like an irrational little turd. Friends will attest to it. Anyway, the word was that they had a spit.

'Beef,' Ross fired back.

Just a bit about Ross Trimboli. Like most pedigreed crims with half a brain, Ross was seriously driven and supremely organised. His days were hectic. He'd meet one or two associates in the morning, do a quick cannabis deal for twenty grand, root two sheilas over lunch, take a meeting, organise a coke deal for the weekend, have a few drinks at the Ex-Servicemen's Club in town, and then his big curly mullet would hit his little pillow for a few hours. If there was a criminal dollar to be turned, Ross was in there tossing the gold coin.

Ross had his weaknesses too. Loved to talk himself up. This meant that his ego needed constant feeding. I was guilty of throwing him a few scraps at mealtime too: 'Jeez Ross, I don't know how you pack it all in. You're a fucken machine.'

On this occasion I replied 'Great' to the confirmation of beef on the spit at Tony's place. 'So, this car's definitely mine in a couple of months, hey Ross?'

After smiling for an instant at Ben Gleeson's trademark chutzpah, Ross then clumsily checked himself, his face growing sober. It was like he suddenly remembered something more important. The whole performance was so forced that it made me kind of jump inside.

He then buzzed his electric window, his poodle head stretching out in the breeze. After coughing up a fresh one, he let fly with a skyward speculator into the Griffith air. Gastronomic housekeeping officially over, he then parked his size-five slipper onto the accelerator.

I looked casually into the side rear-view mirror. Mark's Corolla was fast becoming a speck. This was a surprise. Although the Porsche was obviously no slouch, Ross was no speed demon. Didn't want to shit in his own back yard, so to speak.

'You know, brother Ben, we've got to be careful,' he finally remarked, obeying the speed limit in the process. Mark thankfully loomed larger behind us.

'Why's that?'

'There's undercovers around.'

Interesting. I got a little charge of adrenaline wondering where this conversation was heading. But with that rush, some of the fear returned. 'Yeah, but they're always around, Ross. You know that. We're smart enough to work out who's who.'

'Yeah, but some of the family in Mildura got done by them a couple of years ago,' he replied. 'We must be careful, brother Ben.'

Holy fuck. He floored me with that one. I took it that those Mildura family members were Operation Bert's Matt Medici and Patty Condro.

'You know, those boys got sucked in. The undercover was good. He didn't talk or act like a cop,' he said, eyes fixed on the road before glancing over at me. 'He had long blond hair. He was young.'

Holy, holy fuck. Ross had just described me to a tee. My hair was ponytail length — a little shorter than on the Mildura job, but long and blond all the same. Although I had just turned twenty-six, I looked much younger. They didn't christen me 'The Kid' on Operation Bert for nothing.

I collected myself. 'Yeah, they're a bunch of arseholes. Mate, look, it doesn't take much to, you know, work out who's fair dinkum and who's not. We know what's going on.'

'This is family I'm talking about, brother Ben. I don't think you understand.'

Bloody family. Ross was always banging on about family. But it did ram home one fact: you weren't just trying to nab one bloke, you were trying to bring down a whole bunch of the fuckers.

And everyone was family, no matter how tenuous the genetic correlation. I was quietly hopeful that Medici and Condro were more likely inbred fourth cousins, half a dozen times removed.

Actually, Ross's own spot in the Mafia 'family tree' was an interesting one in itself. He was an underling of the alleged Australian Mafia number one, Vincenzo Spano, and the number two man, Spano's son-in-law Tony Romeo. Yet sometimes the bloke found it difficult to swallow that organisational fact: 'Tony and I are both equals. You know that, don't you, brother Ben?' He would say this to me not so much as a question, more a clamouring for respect. There was a stench of desperation about it too. He must've thought if he said it often enough, it might actually come true.

I never challenged Ross when he tried to flex his muscles this way, but everyone knew the score. Even to the most casual observer, Ross Trimboli was one rung lower on the organised crime food chain than Tony Romeo. But it made me silently snicker to see that whenever Tony told him to do something, Ross would disappear for a quiet sulk. Still, I was always on my toes. After all, the man was only a couple of professional hits away from Godfather status himself.

'Yeah, I understand, Ross. It's family,' I said, maybe a little too disinterestedly.

'Maybe you don't. This hurt our family. This embarrassed our family. Can you understand that, brother Ben?'

'Yeah, I know what you mean.'

'I hope you understand,' he said. 'I really do.'

Before I had a chance to work out what in the fuck that was all about, Tony Romeo's big, showy house thankfully entered our sights. 'This is the joint, isn't it, Ross? Beauty, I'm bloody starving.'

The Porsche came to a halt out the front of Tony's monument to money and very little else. It was the first time I'd seen Casa Romeo in the daylight, and the brown brick palace was quite a sight. Big block, state-of-the-art security with all the trimmings. Frankly, I wasn't impressed. It looked like a huge eighties display home designed for drug dealers on the make.

Ross buzzed his window and reached out to point towards the driveway, indicating to Mark behind us that he should enter first. The Corolla edged past slowly onto the property. I guessed that we were waiting to park behind him.

I guessed wrong. As Mark disappeared from view through Tony's gates, Ross floored it, and we were out of there. Before I knew it we were racing away from Tony's house, away from Mark, back on the road. The Porsche was on the highway before Mark had even wised up that his partner was elsewhere.

Okay, what did we have here? No police cover, and Ross Trimboli had kidnapped me. I'd never been kidnapped before, so I was a little confused as to how I should act.

'Hello Ross, where we going?'
'Don't worry about it, brother Ben,' he laughed.
'Come on, Ross. I'm bloody starving. What's going on?'
'Don't worry about it. We're just going for a drive.'
'Yeah, but where?'
'I want to show you something.'

He'd picked a fine time for show and tell. No wire, no back-up and no gun. Inside, I was unravelling. 'No worries. Do you want to talk to me about something?'

'I'll talk to you soon. When we get there,' he said firmly.

I had no comeback. For the first time in three months, Ross Trimboli was giving me the silent treatment. I was generally pretty good at getting people to tell me things, but not this time. Ross really didn't want to talk.

At the very least, I had some thinking time. What did I know here? I knew that Ross was acting weird again. I knew that his organisation was paying off people in high places who could readily obtain information about our true identities. And, possibly worst of all, I knew that a few blokes I'd put away for drug trafficking in Mildura two years ago were part of his extended family.

What didn't I know? I didn't know if someone had flashed him a photo of me. I didn't know if Mark was on the main course back at Tony's barbecue. And I didn't know if Ross was going to serve me up as tiramisu, if you know what I mean.

The car finally pulled into a farming property in Hanwood, ten minutes north of Griffith. 'This is my house,' Ross explained as we eased our way up the driveway.

My fear was pushed to one side for a moment as I copped a look at the ugly blemish Ross liked to call his digs. Imagine a modest brown brick veneer joint from an outer metropolitan suburb. And then imagine it transported to an environment like the Aussie bush. Taste was in seemingly short supply up Griffith way.

'Fuck, it's nice.' I couldn't help myself enjoying a laugh on the inside at Ross's expense. 'What are we doing here, though?'

'I've got something for you.'

'No worries.'

We both hoisted ourselves out of the Porsche. Before I knew what was going on, Ross walked towards me, lifted my T-shirt and patted me down. The movement was so quick and decisive that if I had been carrying a gun or wearing a wire, I would've been powerless to stop him.

My first thought: *I'm so glad I'm not carrying my gun.* My next thought: *Why didn't I bring my fucking gun?*

'Got anything on ya?' he asked.

'Nah,' I answered, still stunned.

I did know one thing though — pulling a gun on Ross Trimboli was not really an option anyway. Operation Afghan had become so wide-ranging and so promising that the situation would have to be totally black or white. Here

Undercover

we were looking at a grey area, with the distinct possibility of a change of shade down the track.

'Look, what's the problem, Ross?'

'Come with me.'

I stepped into line next to him. 'What do you want to show me? I really am hungry, you know.'

No answer. Ross was elsewhere, in some place I didn't want him to be. His empty gaze was focused solely on the horizon. I didn't know what he could see there, but he sure liked the look of it. The prick was almost smiling.

We then entered an orchard to the rear of the property. 'What is this place?'

'My orange farm,' he answered.

Ross's behaviour changed again. The calmness of a moment ago was gone. Now he started fidgeting. It was like he was waiting for something to happen. Did he think I was about to bust him? Was he expecting my Special Operations Group mates to jump out of nowhere and put a commando death-grip on him? I guess he thought if he were going to be busted by the cops, it would be the perfect time and place.

The path between the trees then narrowed, making it difficult for the two of us to walk side by side. 'Walk in front of me,' he barked.

My stomach turned. And it wasn't a hunger pain. I'd seen this scenario played out on film a thousand times before. *Walk in front of me, loser. Here, have a bullet in the back of your head, loser.*

Under normal circumstances I probably would've refused his invitation, but the path was so cramped that it didn't seem like the most ridiculous request. At least he didn't hand me a shovel, so I fell into line a few steps ahead of him.

'You'd tell me if something was wrong, wouldn't you, Ross?'

'Of course,' he replied.

And so began the slowest, eeriest procession of my life. Orange trees floated in the breathless air to both sides of us. Each shuffled footstep was amplified, and only 50 metres into our Sunday stroll, I felt like I'd been walking for an hour.

This definitely wasn't my preferred choice of death. I mean, if I had to go in this sort of situation I'd want to go down fighting, if nothing else. I considered stopping, but I couldn't jeopardise the whole operation just yet. I had to do something though.

'Why am I fucking walking in here, Ross? Shouldn't we be back at the barbecue?' I said, frustration getting the better of me.

'Just keep going, brother Ben,' he replied, in a sharper tone this time.

I started to question whether the fear was real or not. Maybe it was paranoia. But then the tightness in my stomach would kick in, hoping he wouldn't do anything while we were walking. I was listening for gun sounds or clicks, rustling in his pants, anything.

And then I heard something stir from behind. A sort of fumbling or clutching movement. 'Keep going. We're nearly there,' he said.

I turned around quickly. 'This is a great place,' I said, desperately trying not to sound desperate. I probably sounded desperate. Nothing was in his hands, but his eyes were still checking out that horizon for all it was worth. The prick couldn't even look me in the eyes.

The fear got to me then. My focus kind of switched off. In a way, I'd given up. Rightly or wrongly, it was my usual defence mechanism when things became too tense. So, even though I was terrified, some peace took hold of me.

Maybe it was cowardice on my part, but I just didn't know how to handle it. I had too much pride to risk this job if I happened to be reading the wrong signals. No amount of training could've prepared me for what was happening. I'd tried talking to him, but there was no response. Just that vacant I'm-looking-elsewhere stare. And that really unnerved me the most, because he was completely into what he was about to do.

We then arrived at a group of trees clustered in front of us. The path had trailed off, and we were at an impasse. I stopped reluctantly, waiting for Ross's directions.

'Kneel down, brother Ben.'

Fuck. Yep, this was it. Down on my knees, and a bullet in the back of my head. I just stood there, frozen.

'Kneel down,' he repeated, strangely calmer this time.

Fuck it. I slid down onto my knees, ever so slowly. I was convinced he had a gun in his hands, and I couldn't bring myself to look around to check if my instincts were correct. There was no way I'd have given him the satisfaction of seeing me truly fearful. I just waited. Waited for the bullet to crash into my skull. Seconds passed.

'What now?' I asked, totally submissive.

'In there.'

'In there, what?'

'Just look through there. Straight ahead.'

I couldn't see anything in the darkness that was the clump of trees ahead of me. Not while I was expecting a bullet in the back of my head, anyway. I thought about my poor mum. She'd never find out what happened to me. They'd just dispose of the body, never to be discovered. Another Donald Mackay.

Damian Marrett

I had completely succumbed to the situation. I had completely succumbed to Ross Trimboli. Just waiting to cop one in the head while I was down on my knees. Why wasn't I fighting? I'm a fucken coward. I fucken knew it. Well, come on then, you gutless piece of shit, pull the fucken trigger.

'In there,' he said again.

I didn't move at all. I wasn't going to make it easier for him with me leaning forward, head down. I refused to give him the satisfaction.

'Can you see it?' he asked.

What was he talking about? He was dragging this execution out for all its worth. I craned my neck inside the cranny, but still came up short.

He then reached over my shoulder. It made me physically jump. He started scrounging around, and pulled something out of the cubbyhole. It looked like three large garbage bags. Three garbage bags presumably full of cannabis.

'It's a gift for you, brother Ben,' he said, now smiling a little, like he was expecting some gratitude for his good turn.

Oh my God. A gift? You bet it fucking was. It was the best fucking gift of all.

Relief washed over me like a long hot shower. My whole life had just been given back to me. I wanted to burst into tears, and I had to exercise every last bit of control to avoid doing it. I felt so clean. So very squeaky clean. Like I was ten years old again. Just been showered, and in my dressing gown without a worry in the world. I was an innocent little kid again.

'Great. Right. Nice one, Ross. This is the twelve pounds, yeah?' I asked. This was the end product of our cannabis negotiations from a few weeks ago. I took it that this was his preferred delivery method for first-time deals.

He just nodded and continued to smile.

I picked up the dope, grinning like a ten year old, and then took one of the shortest walks in history back to the car.

On the return drive, Ross was up to his old tricks, talking a million miles an hour again. But I wasn't all there. What the fuck had just taken place? He must've known he was scaring the shit out of me. Everyone knows how the Mafia operate. When a Mafioso orders another man to walk in front of him in the middle of nowhere, it's generally *ciao baby*, I would've thought.

Ross Trimboli had played a game with me, some sort of test. I would have passed too. A copper would never kneel down so willingly in front of a bloke like that. Then again, neither would a crook. He had his reasons for scaring me, but I just wasn't sure what they were.

He could've easily killed me. Just down on my knees, ready to be blown away like a weak prick. I had too much pride to fuck up the job, although I guess he had one over me now. I despised him for it. And, worst of all, I despised myself.

That was my first drive in a Porsche. They're not all they're cracked up to be.

Twelve

March 20-22, 1994

Tony Romeo's front door was open a fraction when Ross and I belatedly lobbed onto his doorstep for the barbecue. So much for his state-of-the-art security. I could just make out the faint rumblings of a small gathering out the back, and the faint rumblings of a ravenous stomach down below. Ross swaggered confidently into the foyer, a relieved Ben Gleeson tailing him. From out of a corridor leading to the living area, Tony Romeo was the first to spot us.

'Brother Ben, you have returned.'

I grinned. 'Yeah, and I'm bloody hungry.'

Tony smiled at my typical disrespect. He was warming to it, in fact. 'Come with me, Ben. There's something I've been meaning to show you.'

Jesus, not bloody again. These Mafia cocksuckers were big on the surprise show and tell. This time I made sure I walked a few paces behind.

'Take a look at this, brother Ben,' Tony said as we approached a purpose-built glass cabinet. Inside was a magnum of champagne. 'This is my 1966 bottle of Dom Perignon. It was given to me for my first Communion, you know, brother Ben?'

'Yeah, yeah, Tony. I'm a Mick too.'

'Good, good,' he replied, his hand on my shoulder. Tony was quite affectionate to me throughout Operation Afghan. I felt as though he genuinely liked me. I'm not sure why.

Maybe because I cracked lame jokes when he least expected it. 'It's worth a lot of money, you know.'

'Yeah, I don't doubt it. We'll have to pop the cork on it one night. Maybe the night I marry your daughter.'

I was sailing a bit close to the wind on that one, but Tony knew me as a cheeky little shit. Sure, Tony's sixteen-year-old daughter was a good sort, but I knew that I would never be considered future son-in-law material.

True to form, his pained reaction (with a hint of disguise) said as much. Imagine the thought of an Anglo outsider hooking up with his Calabrian flesh and blood! Still, my remark wasn't made out of disrespect; I saw it more as a compliment.

'We may be waiting a long time then, brother Ben,' he finally said.

'Yeah, you could be right,' I smiled, looking down the corridor to try to catch a glimpse of Mark. After everything that had happened, a friendly and familiar face was important to me. 'Where's everyone else?'

'Out back,' Tony replied as we continued on our way towards the guests.

Upon entering the living room I was overjoyed to spy Mark grasping a goblet of red wine in the corner, casting an educated eye over Tony's bookshelf. Dignified as ever, the man *was* an art dealer. All he needed was a monocle and a hyphenated surname. But it looked like the whole episode had shaken up the shade of his face. Even though he'd quaffed a few vinos, his cheeks were colourless. He looked as relieved to see me as I did him.

I made my way over, Tony not far behind. 'Ben, you're back,' Mark said, exaggerating his vowels.

'Yes, Mark. I'm back,' I said.

'Where did you get to?' he asked.

'Just looking at a few oranges,' I said as Tony appeared by my side with a glass of Griffith red.

I guess I *had* been looking at a few oranges in Ross's grove, although in this context Mark knew I was really talking about drugs; 'oranges' just happened to be one of our code words for pounds of grass. 'Paintings' was another. It wasn't unusual. Crooks always spoke in code over the telephone in case of intercepts and bugs. During Afghan we also referred to cocaine as 'Picasso'. A typical deal negotiation over the phone might play out something like this: 'Yeah Ben, I've got some more oranges for you to look at, and I'm seeing my man next week about that Picasso you were after.' Frankly it all sounds a bit stupid now, but it made sense to us at the time.

'Brother Ben, come with me for a moment,' Tony said, halfway to the back door before I had a chance to answer. Here we go again.

I followed him outside. 'What is it, Tony?'

'Are you comfortable taking the dope back down to Melbourne?'

'Comfortable? Yeah, yeah, shouldn't be a problem.'

'It's just that I wouldn't throw it in the boot like it is, you know what I mean. Pack it very tightly in another garbage bag or two.'

'Sure.'

'That way the smell, you know, the fumes,' he said.

'No, that's fine.' He was worried that if we were pulled over by the police, the cannabis stench would be easily detected. It was comforting to know that Tony was concerned for our safety. Protective people are good targets. It usually means that they're buying your cover story. But by no means were his motives altogether altruistic. He was probably worried that, if I was caught with the dope, I'd dob him in.

Undercover

'And stick to the speed limit too. You don't want any reason to get pulled over. Everything will be fine then.'

'Yep, no worries. Thanks for that, Tony. I appreciate it.'

'Well, no one wants any trouble.'

There was an uncomfortable silence. We both stood there wondering what to do about it. I then filled up the space as best I could.

'So, when are we eating?' I asked, sussing out the action through the glass doors into the house. All the women were milling around the kitchen, preparing to feed the men in their lives. We were probably five or ten minutes away from chow-time.

'Should be soon,' said Tony as we rejoined the party. I made a beeline for Mark while Ross intercepted Tony at the door. For the first time since my walk through the orange grove, I was alone with my partner.

'Shit, Ben, where the fuck have you been?' Mark blurted out in a half-whisper.

'Mate, I'll tell you later, but I'm happy to report that Ross has come good on that twelve pounds of grass.'

'Fuck, I've spent the last hour thinking you were dead. I was so sick I couldn't talk to anyone. I'd just about convinced myself, you know.'

'To tell you the truth, I'm still getting over the whole bloody thing.'

'Where's the gear now?' he asked.

'It's at Ross's. We'll have to pick it up on our way home.'

'What did he want just then?' he asked, nodding towards Tony. I could tell that the little pep talk I'd just had with the Australian Mafia's number two man had been eating away at Mark for the last few minutes. One thing about Mark Gleeson — he always wanted to be included.

'Nothing, really. Just told me to be careful on the drive home with the dope in the boot.'

'Nice of him.'

Minutes later we all tucked into the food. After a good hour of pigging out on beef and wine, Mark and I retreated to the back yard for a quiet chat. Brothers cum business partners can do that without looking too conspicuous.

Mark filled me in on his side of the ledger. As Ross sped off a greeting party, led by Tony, met Mark in the driveway. After inquiring as to my whereabouts, Tony flippantly brushed it off, telling him not to worry: 'No problems at all, Mark. Ross is just taking Ben for a drive. Come inside. I'll fix you a drink.'

For an hour, Mark was thinking I was in for it; that both our covers had somehow been blown. He was thinking all the same things as me, but without Ross Trimboli acting like a zombie behind him.

It was only natural that Mark had felt just as exposed. No one could've seen it coming, and the stakes were high. Even though both of us had faith in our respective abilities, the uncertainty of the situation was enough to make anyone worry. For Mark, who was unused to working in a covert capacity, even more so.

'Have you ever made your own sausages before, brother Ben?' asked Tony Romeo, at the head of the table at Benson's restaurant.

'Um, not lately.'

He was confused. Probably just trying to work out if I'd been a butcher in a past life. I figured some qualification was required: 'Um, when I said not lately, I kind of meant never.'

'Okay,' Tony replied slowly, after a few seconds of consideration, the unsolved mystery now explained.

'Tomorrow we have a day out at my father-in-law's. It's a picnic, a barbecue, you know. We make sausages. You and Mark must come. Have a go for yourselves. It's a very special day.'

'Sure, Tony. We'd love to.'

By March 1994, Operation Afghan was flying. The plan to import one tonne of marijuana from New Guinea was a real goer, the one-kilo deal of cocaine was close to fruition, and now our Griffith social calendar was filling up. First Ross wanted us to lace up our drinking boots in a week's time, and now an invite to Vincenzo Spano's home the next day. It promised to be an important event.

Most observers identified Spano as Australia's Mafia boss, *numero uno* in Calabrian parlance. In his seventies, Spano was ostensibly retired, but he still barked a few orders when he saw fit. Having said that, the day-to-day running of the business had been deferred to Tony Romeo years ago. Spano lacked the energy and drive required for the top job, and his son-in-law was more comfortable with the vagaries of the modern world. But if Spano arced up about something, no family member would go against him. He had respect, more than total autonomy.

So the next morning Mark and I were primed to manipulate meat at Vincenzo Spano's house. Once again we weren't wired or tooled up for a social occasion like this one, so we jumped into the Corolla for a Sunday sausage. Approaching the Spano house, the size of it surprised me. A Griffith farmhouse of some fifty years' standing, it was nowhere near as ostentatious as Tony Romeo's palace.

Our first stop was the sausage machine, located in a basement underneath the house. Once we entered, the scene before us was peculiar to say the least. Half a dozen blokes were milling around the front of the machine, trying to tease an even flow of mince into its casing. This kind of carry-on was certainly unfamiliar to my eyes.

'Mark, brother Ben, come in,' said a smiling Tony.

'So, this is where the magic happens,' I said, waving my arms like a model on *The Price is Right*.

'Boys, meet my father-in-law. Ben and Mark, this is Vincenzo.'

We both shook the old man's hand, but he didn't utter a word. He didn't need to: his eyes said it all. They were a rich chocolate colour, the likes of which I'd never seen before. There was real depth to them. Like they'd seen the world three times over. Although we came from opposite sides of the fence, it was obvious his whole demeanour commanded respect.

'Would you like to have a go?' asked a gleeful Tony, nodding towards the sausage machine. I'd been expecting this. He viewed us as the day's entertainment — a couple of loser Aussies who not only ate crap sausages, they also bought them from the supermarket. Let's set them loose on the machine and see how they shape up.

'Sure, that's what we're here for.'

Mark and I slotted in next to Domenic Trimboli, prepared to get our hands meaty. My job was to catch the mince in the skin as it oozed out of the machine. There was an art to it, and I was no artist. I discovered quickly that if you didn't pack the sausage evenly it would quickly splatter out the sides, producing more than a few laughs from the experts on the sidelines.

During the process, Mark was his ebullient self. 'This is just fantastic. Do you guys do this often?'

Spano nodded. 'Yes, good family day,' he replied in broken English.

'Well, this to me is what family's all about. Great, great.

Undercover

Family is so important. We're honoured to be here. Thank you, Vincenzo.'

Jesus, Mark could lay it on thick at times. Maybe that's a bit harsh, but I'd copped the customary earful on the way to the Spanos' about the importance of the day.

It was his usual drive-time hassle: 'Now Ben, it's a great honour to be invited today, and I don't want anything to go wrong. We have to show respect for the family.'

As a Detective Sergeant, Mark out-ranked me as a police officer, but I was thoroughly sick of hearing the same old tune. It was understandable — with the amount of time we'd spent together, I guess we'd become like an old married couple. But what did he expect me to do — take a crap in the Spano birdbath?

After ten minutes of trying to collar pork products in a condom, I was relieved of my duty. I had three sausages to my name. Pretty piss-poor effort on the sausage-sculpting front, so I ducked outside for a quiet cigarette. Mark followed soon afterwards.

'That was just sensational, wasn't it, Ben? What tradition! You do realise that no one's ever been invited into this world before, don't you?'

'Yeah, pretty special, I guess,' I said, drawing back heavily on a Wills Super Mild. To be truthful, Mark was beginning to disagree with me. Existing in each other's pockets for months at a time was taking its toll on my patience. And when you're living a lie for what feels like each and every single moment of the day, relationships tend to become even more strained. It was annoying being around him, and I'm sure he felt the same way towards me.

'You do realise the gravity of this situation, Ben?' he asked, lowering his voice. 'We've been invited to a tradition no other copper will ever again be invited to.'

'Yeah, yeah.'

'We're miles from cover, too. I'm getting no phone reception.'

'I know.'

I took another drag of my smoke and scuffed the ground. I didn't need another of Mark's friendly reminders that heavy shit was going down. Yes, we were out of police range, but it appeared that there were plenty of things that Mark wanted to remind me about, most of them worrying.

'Just imagine for a moment what's been through that machine before,' he said. 'It just doesn't bear thinking about.'

'Yeah well, as long as we're not next, huh.'

'This is such an honour, Ben. You have to be respectful. The magnitude of this day, I'm telling you, it's just unbelievable.'

By this stage of the operation, I was starting to get a better handle on my partner. He was treating Afghan as the big adventure in his life, and he wanted to savour every moment, play it out loud for only me to hear. And that's what pissed me off. I felt like I was his only sounding board.

'Don't just look at this as a barbecue, Ben. This is a test. They're looking at us. They're judging us. If the old man doesn't like us, it's over.'

This conversation was chipping away at my nerves, so I didn't even bother responding to Mark's less-than-amazing proclamation. For me, the biggest test was becoming the time we spent together.

If I was truly being honest with myself, I was quietly losing it. I saw Mark as part of the reason. It had reached the stage where we detested each other. I wanted to explode when I was around him. The six-hour drive to

Undercover

Griffith was torture. The six-hour drive back to Melbourne was more of the same. There was no respite. He was so fucking into this job.

'Just one stuff-up could get us killed,' he would blab. 'It only takes one, you know.'

I spent most of the time looking out the window, holding myself back, cultivating my own little stress tumour, polluting the pit of my stomach. That said, most of the time what he said didn't really bother me. I mean, I wasn't that scared about them coming to get me during or after the job. It was just that I constantly had to listen to Mark saying it.

On top of his paranoia, he was always trying to undermine me, trying to remove me from important situations. One night we were looking at maps of New Guinea and Far North Queensland in our motel room, nutting out the big deal. The Trimboli brothers, Ross and Domenic, were sitting in. I felt it was an important meeting. While Ross and I were deep in conversation, Mark developed a thirst all of a sudden. Told me to get in a beer run for the boys. So now I was his bloody dogsbody. But that was just Mark all over.

Give the man his dues — Mark had done an exceptional job infiltrating the Italians, and in many areas I rated him highly. Tactically he was always on the money; evidence-gathering likewise. I think the biggest problem we encountered was that in some ways we were different, while in others we were dangerously similar. We both wanted to be number one, and we both wanted control of certain situations. This was the constant battle, and it eventually destroyed our friendship.

My job was to think like a drug dealer. Mark thought like a businessman, unused to the high margins involved.

Damian Marrett

He had set himself up as an art dealer. They knew him as that, not as a bloke who knew the ins and outs of buying and selling drugs. That's where I came in. When a deal was being struck, Ross would prefer to talk to me. So when Mark started playing funny buggers and leaving me out of negotiations, it pissed me off.

But it wasn't just Mark giving me grief. Friends and family detected a change in my temperament as well. That's if they saw me at all: the job had consumed me, and I had become very distanced from those previously closest to me. Even my mum called me a grumpy bugger one night. Actually, poor example — she always calls me a grumpy bugger.

Seriously, though, I found it very difficult to connect with my nearest and dearest. I felt like I'd lost them for good. And the people who worked with me weren't much help. They had their own problems — why would they want to hear about mine?

Every three months I would see a psychologist; all undercovers were subjected to a quarterly assessment. He might have been some use to me, but I kept him in the dark. During our sessions, I'd always joke around so much that he had no idea where I was coming from anyway. There was a reason I did this. I was certain that if I told the truth they'd take me off the job.

And the job was everything to me. The only time I functioned was doing this job, and here I was, unhappy doing it. I'd get so wound up. Not really depressed, just shitty at the whole world. Nothing in my life was private. I was paranoid all the time. I started to believe I was being followed and bugged. Hey, maybe I was, but I just didn't want to feel that way. Paranoia's a bloody insidious thing.

Friends couldn't really come to my aid. They were getting married, having kids, buying houses, travelling, enjoying themselves, doing all the things I wanted to do. My Saturday nights were spent with Mr Negative telling me I was going to die.

There was also no way I could have a girlfriend. I know women say they like a bit of mystery in their lives, but shit, there was no mystery about my state of mind. I was falling apart.

The job was consuming a hell of a lot of my time. I'd never been a great sleeper, but I was surviving on just two or three hours' sleep a night. If I wasn't going up to Griffith, I was going through the tapes and doing transcripts. So whenever I wasn't with the crooks, I had to listen to their voices anyway. I had to relive moments over and over again. I was being bombarded with this Griffith shit.

To add even more pressure, Mark was continually fighting with the Rover Taskforce. He wanted to run the investigation as well as work as the undercover operative. That's an operational no-no, and too many people were getting their noses out of joint. The fallout from the friction was affecting my performance.

But I still wanted the operation to be a success, and back at the Spanos' I left Mark outside to rejoin the production line inside. Before I could get my hands on more sausage, Ross Trimboli headed me off.

'Hey, Ben, grab Mark for a second. Let's have a quick chat.'

Ross led us to a bench around the side of the Spano garage, and we sat down three in a row. I lit up another smoke.

'Okay, I should have that coke next week,' he said.

'Great, we can pick that up in Melbourne,' I chimed in quickly, purely for strategic purposes. We wanted to identify the source of the cocaine, and if he was happy with our choice of location, it was odds-on his supplier was Melbourne-based.

'Fine, fine.'

'So is that through Pat?' asked Mark. He was talking about Pat Agresta, the Melbourne man he first followed up to Griffith.

Mark's query could have been interpreted a number of ways. We were simply trying to protect our investment, and Pat had already provided us with samples. A drug buyer's job is to source the best product at the best price. We just wanted to know if the quality was going to be comparable. And besides, as undercover operatives, our job was to find out things that people didn't necessarily want to tell us.

'No, Mark, no. Through another one,' Ross replied.

'Can we firm up that price, then, Ross?' I asked.

'I've told you, brother Ben. It's one-eighty. That way everybody's fixed up, and you still make good money. You know, I want everyone to be happy.'

'So, no chance of that price coming down?' I asked. 'It just seems a bit steep.'

It was a hollow request, but I had to give it a go. Like a real drug dealer, I had to beat him down on price. And, behind the scenes, it was the usual cash starvation problem. Afghan was a joint initiative between the Victoria Police and the National Crime Authority, and both organisations were loath to dole out money they probably wouldn't see again. In fact, when money had to run the bosses were always at us to buy cannabis, not cocaine. It was a whole lot cheaper.

On top of that, I was well aware that I could shop around and get a kilo of coke for maybe $160 or $170 000. But I knew that convincing Ross Trimboli that 160 was *his* going rate was another matter entirely.

Undercover

'No, no, brother Ben. We've been through this,' he said, his hand placed on my shoulder. 'Come on, let's have some lunch.'

And that was that. There was no way I was going to push my luck when we were still a relatively unknown quantity. He was solid. We were buying a kilo of cocaine for $180 000. And lunchtime it was.

Most people's only reference point to the Mafia is Hollywood — the *Godfather* trilogy, Martin Scorsese films, and Tony Soprano's hissy fits. If there's one common ingredient linking these examples, it's a tightknit family, and the Griffith Mafia was no exception. However, the operation was run in a uniquely Australian way. I guess what I'm trying to say is that Vincenzo Spano got the first sausage off the barbie that afternoon.

The 'First Sausage for Spano' principle is just another way of saying that the Griffith Mafia relied very heavily on a pecking order. The natural order of things was drummed into family members from a young age. Not only was the organisation highly structured, it also took care of those who would probably struggle outside the family unit.

Take Tony's brother, Rocco 'Roy' Romeo, as an example. I always suspected he was a bit simple, but as a loyal and trusted footsoldier in the day-to-day affairs of the family business, he was well compensated for his limited and clumsy efforts. I think he got the sixth or seventh sausage that day. Mark and I came in second and third as VIPs, but we would've been prepared to wait our turn. We didn't want to set off World War III over a homespun snag.

Thirteen

MARCH 25, 1994

The next Friday we were back up in Griffith prepared to party, Ross Trimboli-style. Weeks in the planning, Ross was extra-keen to act as our local tour guide. Even before hitting the highway north we had a fair idea of what the night would entail. He'd mentioned in a phone call during the week that he'd organised some girls to 'entertain' us.

That snippet of information complicated and compromised things. Senior Sergeant Andy Brennan of the Rover Taskforce argued that we should pull out of the night's festivities. By his reckoning, coppers shouldn't play around with hookers when they're on the job, so to speak. He had a point.

Our controller, Sergeant Steve 'Coach' Cody, thought differently. Ross has been talking up the night for months, and set in stone weeks earlier. We'd been backed into a corner. To pull out now could risk the operation. In fact, it would've been illogical to pull out now. Imagine the shoddy excuse: 'Sorry, Ross, not up to it tonight. I've got a sniffly nose, Mark needs to nurse me through it, and there's a *Little House on the Prairie* marathon playing on the motel's in-house cable.'

Even if we did come up with a good lie, we were sure that Ross would want to reschedule this night at some stage. What excuse would we come up with the following week? It was another one of his tests, as far as we were concerned.

Undercover

Coach Cody believed we should make the call ourselves. Boss Brennan still clung tight to the high moral ground. Officially he said no to the evening taking place. Unofficially we went ahead with it anyway. The operation was much too important to wimp out over a technicality.

So the evening kicked off at Benson's (veal scaloppini again). The three targets dining with the two of us were Ross Trimboli, Domenic Trimboli and Roy Romeo. No Tony though. I think he was watching *Little House on the Prairie* reruns at the family's motel.

After splurging out on a few rounds of the best cognac post-meal, Ross took care of the bill. It totalled more than $800. Pretty steep, but on top of that, he also tipped the young waitress $200 for her time (and her looks). It paid good money providing a service for Ross; the Griffith economy relied upon him.

After dinner we headed back to the Astra Motel. A room on the fourth floor had been set aside for entertainment purposes. It wasn't particularly plush, but it contained all the elements Ross Trimboli required for a good party: plenty of alcohol, three or four young prostitutes working the room, and a small mound of cocaine resting on the surface of the bar.

'Help yourselves, Mark, brother Ben,' said Ross, nodding at the coke. 'It's there if you want it.'

Mark and I both expected drugs to be on offer because we knew how much Ross loved the stuff. All the same, I didn't take up his offer, sitting down with a Crownie and soaking in the crappy ambience instead. There was no music playing in the background. Just a bunch of blokes sitting around like kings, and a few young women fawning all over them. It was business as usual for Ross, though. Every day he had to have a prostitute.

Unlike Ross, I was far from relaxed or comfortable. The whole scene had a dark edge to it, but maybe it was just my mood that made me think that way. At some stage I knew that I'd be coerced into having sex with a prostitute. No wonder I was so wound up.

I'm no saint (or a prude) but, deep down, the thought of this night had been weighing heavily on my mind since Ross originally raised it. I'd never slept with a prostitute before. In fact, I'd never even considered sleeping with a prostitute before. And although it was just blokes being blokes, I had no desire to break my duck, especially when I considered the ages of the girls. They were young, barely eighteen. I was still in my twenties, but even I thought they were too young. Ross and the boys, well into their thirties, thought differently of course.

In the meantime, Ross cornered the both of us, discussing cocaine and the importation thereof. I asked him how he got so much stuff into the country. He told me that he had a team of females who would bring coke into the country, posing as pregnant women. Apparently they could strap more to their bellies that way. It transpired that most of the family's gear was trafficked into Australia by drug mules but, bear in mind, they were experts at diverting from the truth.

'We know a bloke down at the docks,' Mark said. We'd planned on passing this information along for a while to see if we could get a bite. Now seemed like a perfect time to raise the issue.

'Do you?' asked Ross.

'It's actually Alison's father,' lied Mark. In reality, if need be, we'd use an older covert operative posing as Alison's father.

Throwing Alison's name into the mix was a risk from our perspective. Shunted into the background nearly six months previously, Mark's 'girlfriend' had been good mates with the Griffith gang before I arrived on the scene. In fact, Mark had told Ross that Alison was now his 'fiancée', and that was our problem: Ross was always angling for an invite to the 'engagement party'.

'That's very good to know. People like that are very important, Mark. So, when's the engagement party?' Ross asked, true to bloody form. All the same, the change of subject surprised us. We thought a bent bloke on the docks would be a good contact for someone like Ross Trimboli. The 'pregnant' drug mules sounded like a much bigger gamble.

'It's coming. You'll be the first to be told, Ross, you know that,' replied Mark, almost with a sigh.

'But why the hold-up?' he asked.

This was the risk as far as we were concerned: the job was lasting longer than expected, and Ross wanted an invite to this engagement party. There was a running joke on Afghan that if the operation dragged on much longer, we'd have to put on this shebang ourselves. All the guests would be plain-clothes coppers, except for an unaware Ross and his crew. Imagine the gifts. I still maintain that Ross would've been good for, I don't know, a new car.

'Alison's stressed, you know, getting all the family together, but it'll work out,' replied Mark. 'Soon, yep, soon.'

'That man, Alison's father,' said Ross, thankfully returning to the original conversation. 'Is he in Melbourne?'

'Yeah, sure is. The bloke can organise anything,' said Mark.

'Get in touch with him,' said Ross, finally taking the bait. 'We've got one hundred kilos ready to go in Canada.'

'Coke?' I asked.

'Yes, coke,' Ross confirmed. 'Has he got connections to get it through?'

'Sure,' said Mark.

'Because if he has, I'll send someone to Canada next week and get it here straightaway.'

'I'll let you know,' said Mark with a small hint of weariness. He was probably thinking the same thing as me. Sure, this Canadian import was another angle, but first things first. The New Guinea drug importation was the main game. If we delayed that, this job could prove unmanageable. We'd be working away on these targets for years and years, making the engagement party a distinct possibility. I had a feeling that Alison's father would never be wheeled out.

'Now there was one thing I wanted to ask you, Mark. This plane, does it have two engines?' asked Ross.

'Um, yeah, it's a twin-engine,' I said.

'Good, good. If one engine stops, we must keep going,' he said.

I almost laughed at the absurdity of his statement, but it was obviously something that was causing Ross concern.

But I needn't have worried about holding back the laughs: Mark was pissing himself. 'Yes, two engines, Ross,' he said. 'That I'm sure of.'

'Another thing,' Ross continued, ignoring Mark's belly laugh. 'There's only one customs official on the island, right?'

'Yeah, one,' I said.

'Now, my man in New Guinea tells me this one bloke shouldn't be a problem. We can pay him off easily.'

'Yep, good idea. You'll organise that, yeah?' said Mark.

'Well, that saves a lot of crap,' I said. 'Good shit.'

'Leave it with me,' said Ross. 'My man will take care of all that.'

Undercover

Unofficial business out of the way, Ross then casually introduced one of the girls to me. 'This is Melinda. You take her and make sure you have a good time, brother Ben.'

Melinda didn't need much encouragement. One minute we were being introduced, the next she virtually dragged me over to the couch. I sat down lazily and she nestled into my armpit. It was the moment I had been dreading.

'Do you want to go somewhere more private?' she whispered.

'Yeah, let's go down to my room.'

To be honest, I was happy to get away from everyone. My parties needed some background noise; a few drooling gangsters didn't quite fit the bill.

When we arrived in my room, I headed for the minibar fridge. Reaching for a cold one, this triggered off a fear: I wondered if the room was bugged. Hopefully Domenic Trimboli hadn't installed a video system since his last clumsy effort. I didn't fancy showing my wares to the whole of the Griffith Mafia fraternity on their next buck's night: 'Hey Tony, check out brother Ben's dick. I honestly thought it'd be bigger than that.'

From the outset, it became apparent that Melinda liked to multitask. Her job description clearly involved some espionage work as well. Ross must've worded her up beforehand that he wanted information on Ben Gleeson; as we suspected, it looked like this whole party scenario was another one of Ross Trimboli's tests. This time he thought he'd ply us full of cocaine and alcohol, and see how vulnerable we were when our pants were round our ankles.

'What do you do for a job?' asked Melinda, clinically zipping down her miniskirt to reveal bugger all underneath.

'I renovate houses. What do you do?'

'Hmmm, a lot of things,' she said, a coquettish little smile breaking out across her face. 'You must have a lot of money, hanging around with Ross. Where do you renovate?'

'In Melbourne.'

'Yeah, whereabouts?' This was turning into real twenty-questions stuff. It sickened me that a girl so young could be under Ross's control. He owned her, and I hated that idea.

'Like I said, in Melbourne.'

'I meant whereabouts in Melbourne. Did you grow up there?'

'Yes, yes I did.'

'Have you lived anywhere else?'

Oh God. It was kind of laughable if Ross thought this girl could extract information from anyone. The questions not only lacked subtlety, they were delivered as awkwardly as a crap politician's lie.

'Not really, no,' I answered.

'Is all your family there?'

'Some.'

It was as though she was checking them off one by one. 'How long have you known Ross?'

'Jesus, um, I don't fucken know,' I said, beginning to get the shits up.

'You must have a lot of money to hang out with them?'

I didn't answer that one because I felt pretty sure I'd dealt with it before. It was then that she started to twig that I wasn't the most natural of conversationalists. She then reached back into her bag of tricks one last time, but nothing was there. So we stopped talking.

Sorry, but I won't go into the details. Let's just say that the prostitute-shagging scenario wasn't everything I could have hoped for. It felt dirty. I don't like being forced to do anything, and I wasn't in charge of the situation at all —

hard going for a control freak. And, to be frank, the act itself bored me. I found it difficult to keep my mind on the main game. This pissed me off no end. I knew that the quicker this night was over, the better I would feel. In turn, that made the evening bloody well last forever.

Job done, I returned to the party upstairs. The 'merrymaking' was finishing up. Still no music, the room was even quieter than before. The atmosphere was worse than eerie; it was now frighteningly dark. Everyone was just sitting there, not a word passed between them all. Mark was the only one who looked remotely pleased to see me.

Now that I'd taken care of business (and the girls had grilled us), there was no need to keep up the pretence. The party was over. After a few yawns, Mark and I made our excuses and returned to our room.

'What do you reckon that was all about?' I asked, once we had returned to the relative safety of Room 314.

'What?' Mark replied, pointing to the bar fridge for my benefit. It was a timely reminder that the room was probably bugged, just as I was about spill my guts.

'I don't know,' I said, after a moment collecting myself. 'It's just that little bitch gave me the third degree. Asked me a million and one questions.'

'Mate, don't ask me why she did it. Bloody ask her,' he said.

I walked to the bathroom. Mark didn't follow me. He clearly didn't want to discuss the night, especially considering Domenic's handiwork had possibly been installed. He was probably all talked out after the hooker, anyway.

Shortly afterwards, I tucked myself into bed, annoyed and frustrated that I had to go through what I just went through. And for what? This job was really screwing with my mind. I'd truly had enough.

Damian Marrett

The next day, the two of us slipped out for an early morning coffee on Banna Street. We needed some privacy away from prying eyes. As expected, Mark had also been bombarded with questions. We then knew that Ross's bonking bash was just another test. He wanted to find out more information about the two of us, and who better than a team of prostitutes to play superspy for him? Blokes talk shit when they're coked and boozed up and, if the two of us were coppers, we wouldn't be taking prostitutes to bed. Or so Ross Trimboli believed. I figured I'd passed the test.

Fourteen

April 1994

Early April, and Mark moved out of the East Melbourne apartment. He'd had enough of living in a house with more surveillance equipment than furniture. On reflection, we *had* stacked the joint with devices. When gangsters popped in for a cuppa, the place quickly transformed itself into a television studio minus the technicians.

The main camera was installed inside the tiniest of cracks in the wall above the television. The crack was so small that, from even a short distance, the human eye would have been unable to pick it up. All our Melbourne meetings with Ross Trimboli and co. were conducted in the living room, usually on the couch facing the wall. As a result, we were chalking up plenty of evidence.

The fun and games didn't just stop there. There were about half a dozen microphones hidden in the living room furniture. The phone was 'off', providing a direct line to the Special Projects Unit. A camera was mounted through a crack in the kitchen ceiling, just in case the conversation switched rooms. Even the Milo tin on the kitchen bench contained a microphone installed in a false bottom.

I might add that the technology today is so advanced as to render all this information obsolete. These days, cameras and devices are undetectable, giving agents in the field a distinct advantage. There I go again, sounding like a bloke who had it tougher in his day.

Damian Marrett

Anyway, because we'd invested so much time and money in decking out the house, the moment Mark moved out, I cancelled the lease on my apartment, placed my furniture in storage, and made the place my own.

Once inside, my new life was backstopped to the hilt. The contents of the house gave nothing away as to my true identity. No connection could be made to Damian Marrett. Ben Gleeson was only a few months old, but the apartment was littered with his tax records, correspondence, business cards, car rego, his love letters. A photo of Mark and Alison even sat on top of the telly. About the only thing we couldn't change was the DNA on my toothbrush.

Even though it was time-consuming and expensive, the whole backstopping procedure was essential to the operation. Tony and Ross had already proven themselves to be very surveillance-savvy. Sure, they trusted Mark and his brother Ben, but when there was so much money (and potential jail time) on the line, implicit trust had to be earned.

For that very reason, it came as no surprise when someone rifled through my undies drawer about a week after I'd moved in. Well, not exactly my undies drawer, but it was kind of a relief that the house was broken into. The amount of effort that we'd put into Ben and Mark Gleeson, we were happy for them to take a look around at our stuff. Hopefully it would set their minds at ease.

The break-in job was very professional. Mark noticed some screws had been detached from panelling above the fireplace. They were still screwed in but, on closer inspection, the heads of the screws had no dirt or dust on them, unlike everything else surrounding them. It was just a little thing, but it was also a dead giveaway that they'd been tampered with.

Undercover

They were probably checking for devices behind the fireplace. There was nothing there, so we were happy for them to do that. They would've had to have been extremely thorough in order to discover any trace of our surveillance equipment. Knocking down a wall could prove tricky. Thankfully, they didn't fix themselves a cup of Milo.

A few days later the kilo of cocaine deal was conducted. Ross rang Mark in the morning to let him know that everything was prepared. He was then given specific instructions to meet Ross at the First and Last Hotel on the Hume Highway in Fawkner.

After Mark arrived at the pub, Ross whisked him away to Fifi Romeo's house around the corner. In Fifi's garage the cocaine was revealed to him, stored in a plastic bag. The size of a football, it was wrapped in tinfoil with plastic bags stickytaped around the outside. Mark ripped into it with a Swiss Army knife to check the contents. Everything seemed to be in order.

A phone call was then placed to me back in East Melbourne. A half-hour later, I met Mark in a Fawkner back street. We'd already arranged with Ross beforehand that I'd be testing the purity of the cocaine before buying it. He was happy with that demand so long as Mark stayed with him in the interim. So Mark handed me the coke, and I was away.

What Ross didn't know was that it wasn't the most independent analysis — I used the Victoria Police Forensics Department in Macleod. On the drive there I made good use of my rear-view mirrors. A couple of anti-surveillance manoeuvres later I pulled into the lab, 100 per cent certain no one was tailing me.

After forensics expert Kate Quinn gave me the thumbs up that the cocaine was indeed cocaine, the gear was weighed, photographed, videoed and logged. Now we just had to pay for the stuff.

I'd telephoned Controller Cody on my way to Forensics, so he met me there, handing me a backpack containing the $180 000, a combination of fifties and hundreds, all in bundles of $10 000.

From the lab I went directly back to the apartment, and called Mark first thing. 'Come round. Not a problem.'

Half an hour later, Ross Trimboli knocked on the front door. Mark was with him. I showed Ross into the living room, and stood in between the couch and the camera, ensuring that all the action was captured. I went into the bedroom, and came back with a blue adidas bag.

'So, no problem, brother Ben?' asked Ross, somewhat impatiently. He looked and sounded as though he wanted to be elsewhere. No worries though. I just took it that he was late for another meeting.

'All in order, Ross. Yeah, good stuff,' I said, handing over the bag full of cash.

'Great, everyone's happy. Now, I have to get on the move. We'll catch up for dinner tonight, yeah?'

'Sure, no worries.'

Mark showed him to the door, and it was as simple as that. The deal had been done. When Mark returned, he slumped on the couch, 'You wouldn't believe what just happened to me.'

'What?'

'I asked Ross about Donald Mackay.'

I was all ears. When Mark and I had first discussed our goals for Operation Afghan all those months ago, we'd made a pledge to each other: to do whatever it took to track down the location of Donald Mackay's remains. We figured his widow at least deserved to put the body to rest.

It was important to both of us, and we were kind of evangelical about the whole thing.

We were under no illusions that it was a big ask. Mackay had disappeared in 1977, and painter and docker James Bazely had been put away in 1986 for conspiracy to murder. But that never put a stop to the final resting-place theories. In police circles, the gossip continues to this day. The most popular theory speculated that his bits were put through a sausage machine — a fine Calabrian tradition, as we discovered. Another one intrigued me: a few coppers had been told that his body was stacked on top of another corpse in a grave at Fawkner Cemetery. The underworld's version of a 'two for the price of one' deal. To my way of thinking, it wasn't the most implausible explanation doing the rounds.

'You're joking. What did you say?' I asked.

'The conversation was kind of about the past. Well, it seemed to be heading that way, so I just kind of innocently asked what happened to him.'

'Shit. How did he react?'

'He pretty much told me to shut up. Said they never talked about it.'

'Shit.'

'He then told me to never mention it again.'

'Well, there goes that idea,' I said.

'Yeah well, I thought I'd give it a shot.'

'Nah, it's all right. I just, you know, think we never stood a chance anyway.'

'Probably not,' Mark agreed.

I was also on the end of a similar Ross Trimboli reprimand just a few days later. Mark and I had driven up to Griffith again to put the finishing touches on the proposed New Guinea importation. This time we were out scoping airstrips.

Damian Marrett

On a lazy Sunday drive through southern New South Wales, Ross was riding passenger while I took the wheel. I'm not sure how or why, but Bob Trimboli's name cropped up in general conversation. Ross just touched on him briefly, but stupidly I tried to get him to elaborate. 'What was your uncle like, you know, as a bloke?'

His response was curt and familiar. 'Brother Ben, he was a good man, but we don't talk about those sorts of things.'

I didn't want to push it too far, so I left it at that. We'd learned our lesson. The Griffith Mafia does not like to talk about the past.

Our destination that day was Cohuna, a small Victorian town not far from the Murray River border. About a three- to four-hour drive from Griffith, Ross had been told that the airstrip matched all of our criteria.

Ross had already given us about $15 000 to organise the pilot and plane, the living room camera capturing the moment for the jury to ponder on at a later date. Ross was comfortable with things his end — the New Guinea end — so locating a suitable strip was now at the top of our agenda.

The airfield was about two or three kilometres south of the town proper. The drive there was typically unspectacular, unless you were a fan of car wrecks. Each farm had a shit-heap graveyard accumulating rust in a front paddock.

After we drove through the airfield's gates, we made a few observations. First off, it was secluded and unmanned — two high priorities on our set of conditions. Secondly, it contained a long, well-paved and -maintained tarmac, probably our highest priority. In fact, the Cohuna airstrip was the only one in the immediate area that could sustain over one tonne of weight.

Ross was very impressed by what we'd discovered. Barring any unforseen circumstances, we had ourselves an airstrip to land the cannabis.

Cohuna was roughly halfway back to Melbourne, and the temptation was there for Mark and I to continue south and home. But that evening we were due back in Griffith for a meeting at Tony Romeo's. He wanted to be kept up to speed on the importation's progress.

A few hours later Tony met us at the door of his Griffith house, and it was handshakes all round. Ross had already called him on a mobile to tell him the good news about Cohuna. 'Come through, boys. We'll have a drink to celebrate, yes?'

We walked through to the room housing all the soft leather. Mark took out some maps of Australia and New Guinea, placing them on the floor in front of us. He took out a black pen and circled Cohuna, then all the landing and refuelling destinations on the way back from Horn Island.

'Well, we're ready for that dummy run you wanted, Ross,' Mark said, taking the floor. 'Jimmy can fly us from Essendon Airport all the way to Horn Island.'

'Where do we refuel on the way?' asked Ross.

'Bourke, you know Bourke ... um, Charleville and Cairns in Queensland,' Mark replied.

'We'll meet up with the plane in Cairns for the test run. It's quicker to fly up with Ansett,' said Ross.

'Same with me,' said Mark.

'Okay then, I'll fly up with Jimmy in the Piper,' I said. 'Now, who do we have to pick up in Cairns?'

'Um, there'll be two others with me, I think.'

'That should be fine, Ross. The plane seats seven,' I said.

'Are you coming, Tony?' asked Mark.

'No, no,' replied Tony. 'Ross will take care of it.'

At any available opportunity, Mark and I tried to include Tony in our conversations. Our bosses were mindful of the fact that he preferred to play the quiet type when our tape was rolling. As a result of his reluctance to speak, we were instructed to try to gather more evidence on him. It was tough; he usually let Ross do all the talking. And Ross didn't need any coaxing.

The next day I was dropped back at East Melbourne, my nerves jangling after six hours of Mark reminding me that we were both going to die slow and miserable deaths in the very near future. It was late afternoon, and I didn't want to coop myself up, so I decided to go down to work. When I got there, the office was already deserted. Everyone was off duty.

I didn't want to go back to the apartment by myself, but I had nowhere else to go. On the drive back I was feeling more and more alone, even scared. Emotionally, I felt like I was struggling.

At the apartment, I was no better. In fact, there was a very real and immediate darkness to my mood; a darkness I'd never encountered before. I felt helpless. Cradling my face in my hands, I began to cry. And the tears had purpose to them. They dragged themselves up out of my guts, taking my breath away.

The more I worried, the more I cried. I felt that undercover work had consumed my entire life for two and a half years, and I hadn't achieved anything. Family and friends had all but fallen by the wayside; I couldn't maintain relationships; and if I managed to sleep at night, I had only my gun and nightmares for company.

Undercover

I was totally exhausted. I felt like a child, a lightweight, someone who couldn't cope with the demands of the job. I had become the type of weak person I would normally have no time or respect for.

I then got up off the couch and stumbled to the bathroom. Splashing cold water all over my face, I looked at my reflection: dead and sad. I hated the person I was looking at, so much so that I found myself sliding down the wall behind me, landing on the bathroom floor. For a long time I just sat there, my head pounding, trying to find a positive.

Finally I got to my feet and started pacing the small flat. The voice inside my head was incessant and relentlessly negative. I poured myself a vodka, hoping that alcohol would pick me up. It was a mistake. I continued to sink lower and lower as waves of intense anxiety collapsed on me. My whole world was caving in.

I couldn't stomach the direction my life had taken. My job was to lie to people, then turn their lives upside down. Even sadder, I was good at it. My reward for this talent was the possibility of retribution, accompanied by all of this guilt and loneliness.

It took me a full hour before I finally calmed myself for longer than five minutes. I picked up the phone and called my brother-in-law, a good mate. The line went through to an answering machine. I asked him to call me back. Through no fault of his I was still alone, waiting by the phone, half an hour later.

My thoughts were now going around in circles. There was no way I could sleep, so I decided to take a short walk into the city to catch a movie. I can't even remember which film I saw, but I took a seat in the dark and then partially blacked out. All I remember is shaking, sobbing, pathetically trying to crouch down between my seat and the one in front of me. Like I was trying to get away from my worthless little world. In reality, I had no idea what I was doing. I was just down on the floor, trying to make myself invisible, yet quietly moaning, thinking to myself, 'Oh fuck, what's happening? You're having a breakdown.' I even thought about myself in the second person. It was as though I couldn't take responsibility for the mess I'd become. This could not be happening to me.

'Hey mate, are you okay?'

Someone was approaching me, so I forced myself upright and brushed past him to the exit. I had to get out of there and go home. I'd never felt anything like this before, and I was sure that I couldn't do anything but ride the bloody thing out. When I got home I poured myself a drink, and stared at my pistol sitting on the carpet next to my feet.

My brain was processing everything, but registering nothing that made sense. Difficult to explain now, but the world went so big, and here I was, a small part of it, yet not connected to anything at all.

Still, I managed to try calling one friend who I could trust in such a personal situation. Chris Murphy, my good friend and controller on Operation Bert, had worked long-term undercover jobs in the past. I knew that talking to him would go no further, so I rang his mobile. It was out of range.

This surge of loneliness then swallowed me. I was missing out on the best years of my life, and for what? Was I actually making a difference? Did I actually want to make a difference? Why in the fuck was I doing this job? At that stage, nothing seemed worth it. I was weak. I was pathetic.

Undercover

I felt like I couldn't include anyone in the misery that appeared to be my life. I couldn't tell a workmate. I knew that undercovers had been in this exact situation before, but I always believed that I was above that sort of thing. It sounds stupid now, but my arrogance was very well developed.

My mind couldn't focus on reality at all. I thought about my family. My fucked-up mind was telling me that they didn't care about me anyway. It was crazy, but all my reasoning was malevolently motivated and suicidal in its intent. It didn't help that I was still drinking straight vodka, either. And next to the bottle was my semiautomatic pistol. Just lying there.

It was all so convenient. I slowly picked up the gun. At first I just held it for a while, not quite believing what this seemed to be leading up to. I then placed the barrel in my eye socket, breathing heavier, my finger tight on the trigger. I wanted to end it all.

I started putting pressure on the trigger, squeezing down on it bit by bit. I braced myself, knowing that there were only millimetres in it. And then, something gave. I burst into tears, releasing pressure on the gun, collapsing to my side on the couch. I immediately felt sick about what had nearly happened, and I didn't pick the gun up again that night.

The next morning, I woke up in my bed. Fragments of the previous night's madness formed a demented slide show in my mind. It wasn't the best viewing, but besides the hangover, I felt much better. For one thing, I was pretty sure that the worst of what I had was over. I'd bottomed out.

I walked into the living room, and the pistol was still lying on the couch. I was quietly pleased with myself that I hadn't brought the thing to bed with me. It was a good decision, considering I had a habit of sleeping with my gun every night.

But the temptation must have been there. I knew that I'd been deadly serious the night before. I wasn't just testing myself. If it hadn't been for the people who would have been affected by my action, I could have easily pulled the trigger.

In the job, I'd had experience with plenty of suicides. Every uniformed copper knows what I'm talking about. Most that I attended had one thing in common: no one expected them to do it. They were always easygoing, never had a care in the world. In some respects, that description fit me.

From that point on, and for the most part, outwardly I was fine. Inside I was a misery, but I would laugh and carry on regardless. Nobody ever detected what felt like a huge weight I was carrying. What a waste of time and energy it all seems to me now, but at that moment I felt like a failure. I wasn't an undercover's arsehole.

So that's what two and a half years of continual undercover work did to me. I still can't believe that I did another three and a half after that. For years, the remnants of that night stayed in me. I'm only thankful that I've never felt that same way again.

Of course, no one knew about that night or the fallout from it. I would've been taken straight off the job and, at that time, I happened to be well entrenched in the biggest operation of my career. It was nearing completion, so for the time being I knew that I had to chuck on the happy face.

It took me quite a while to return to normal. Over the course of the next few years I began to appreciate life a little bit more, to stop punishing myself unnecessarily. One of my perceived strengths was assessing a situation, and then predicting where it would head. Finally, I assessed that I was heading six feet under. Actually, thinking about it now, it's probably not one of my strengths. It took me three or four years to cotton on.

Fifteen

May 1994

'So will they have guns?'

The question was asked by our wide-eyed pilot, Jimmy. He wasn't concealing the fact that he was harbouring second thoughts before the dummy run to Horn Island. His query, hopefully not prescient if things turned awry, came towards the end of a briefing at an empty office space in East Melbourne which we used as a safe house. Others present at the meeting included Sergeant Steve 'Coach' Cody, Senior Sergeant Andy Brennan, and brothers Mark and Ben Gleeson.

'Nah, wouldn't think so, buddy,' Coach said. 'I mean, there'd be no reason for them to tool up.'

Coach was keeping Jimmy's mind on the job. We all knew that Ross carried a gun. Probably slept with one under his pillow. If we were being totally honest with Jimmy, there'd be no reason for anyone on the plane not to come tooled up, the Gleeson brothers included.

Actually, it had become a delicate process dealing with Jimmy. On one hand, we didn't want him to live in fantasyland by giving him the impression that the operation was a piece of piss. On the other, we didn't want to freak out the bloke with talk of guns, drugs and grisly deaths, followed by a quick mince through a Griffith sausage machine. Let the bloke worry about the flying, not the dying.

Undercover

A few days before the briefing, Jimmy had expressed reservations about his role in the operation. He was seriously thinking about pulling out. Coach even had to talk to him privately. It was understandable for a stable bloke in his late forties to question his involvement. His desk job at the Coroner's Court didn't exactly set the pulse racing — it was probably a major catastrophe if a dead body fell off a slab. Imagine the turmoil if dead bodies started falling out of planes.

'They're not gonna talk to me, are they?' Jimmy asked Coach, his chubby red cheeks puffed out. 'You know, I just don't want to talk to any of them.'

'We'll tell them that, no problems,' replied Coach. 'You just concentrate on flying the thing, mate. Whack on the headphones, put on some sunnies, you know, enjoy yourself.'

The week before, Jimmy had spent the good part of an afternoon with Mark formulating a cover story. It was established that they'd met at a party fifteen years ago. Jimmy had taken Mark for a few joyrides over the years. They'd kept in contact through a mutual friend. That was about the strength of it. Sometimes the best cover stories are brief. Let others fill in the blanks.

But Jimmy didn't like brief. 'What if they ask what school I went to?'

'Tell them,' said Mark.

'What? Just tell them?'

'Why not?'

'I don't know. Shouldn't I have a school ready to tell them?' asked Jimmy.

'Scotch College. There you go — Scotch College. Tell them you went to Scotch.'

'Nah, I don't know anything about Scotch.'

And on and on it went. After the meeting, Coach got a phone call from a confused Jimmy. His brief cover story had become the opposite of brief. It was now so large that it bordered on unworkable. After Coach scaled it back down to skin and bone for him, Jimmy was once again prepared to board the plane with us.

Two days after the final briefing (and a week after Jimmy's reservations), everything was in readiness for the dry run. Surveillance had already loaded up the aircraft with a bunch of devices. Microphones were installed into the interior walls, and a camera was located behind a crack to the rear of the plane — small enough to go unnoticed, but large enough to capture the whole plane's belly.

The plan was to fly to Cairns and meet up with the rest of the passengers, who were flying there domestically on a 747. I was flying the friendly skies in the Piper with the fully headphoned and sunglassed Jimmy. Alongside the two of us, or at least behind us, was controller Coach Cody.

Of course, being a behind-the-scenes man, Coach wasn't going all the way to Cairns to meet our targets. He was hitching a ride to Innisfail (about an hour's drive south of Cairns), where he had to liaise with the Queensland Police about the operation. Seeing as we were whizzing through their airspace, it would be considered poor form not to fill them in on the whole affair. We wouldn't mind their assistance either. Plus if something went wrong on the dummy run, Coach would be a lot closer to the action in Innisfail.

We weren't long in the air before I twigged that I had drawn the short straw. The Piper was to the 747 what AC/DC are to Bob Dylan unplugged. Yep, the Piper was a noisy little bugger. The eardrums copped a merciless flogging from go to whoa, and you had to shout to be heard. Not only would we be in the air for fourteen hours, but I was also aware that the listening devices would be flat out picking up general conversation when our targets jumped on board.

As intended, we refuelled the plane at Bourke and Charleville. Next stop Innisfail, where we waved goodbye to Coach. Just half an hour later we landed at Cairns Airport, with only our final destination of Horn Island to go.

The plan for the two of us was to stay with the plane and, after refuelling, wait for Mark to locate us. He did so in less than ten minutes. Following behind him on the tarmac were Ross and two others.

'Hey, fellas. Jump on board,' I said, helping the four of them up the stairs and into the plane. Mark was first. A sweaty Ross came second, dressed to kill in a suit that didn't quite fit him right. It was hot outside, probably more than 30 degrees Celsius. I could tell the suit was giving him the shits — he was literally itching to get out of it.

'Ben, this is Ali, our man from New Guinea,' Ross said, scratching his lower back.

Ali was a tall, dark-skinned bloke, over six foot. 'G'day mate,' I said. He laughed nervously for some reason as he ducked his head on entrance.

'And this is Jim, Jim Alfonso,' said Ross. 'He's looking after the New Guinea end of things.'

I looked Alfonso in the eyes and shook his hand firmly. He looked familiar. I knew the guy, or I thought I did. I wasn't sure where from, but I panicked a little bit. Fortunately he only glanced at me, and in the confusion of introductions I'm sure that my panic didn't register with him. But I had just about convinced myself that I somehow knew a member of Ross's extended family.

And this was a situation I could do without — stuck 10 000 feet in the air and my cover blown. If it came to that, I knew that there was no way out of it; I would have nowhere to go. Whatever played out, I'd just have to hang in there. Or maybe grab a parachute as I made my way to the door.

Everyone was then introduced to Jimmy the pilot. Or, more precisely, Jimmy's back. He was fussing over the instruments like a man who had flying on his mind, not guns and drugs and grisly deaths followed by a quick mince through a Griffith sausage machine. Up the front of the plane, he looked the flying ace: headphones were attached; sunglasses were mirrored. Even though he had his back turned to the passengers when introduced, he still gave them the courtesy of a wave.

That interlude over, my mind went back to familiar Jim Alfonso. I cautiously glanced towards him while he struggled with his hand luggage. I still couldn't place his face, but I took solace in the fact that this wasn't the most unusual dilemma for an undercover operative. On any given operation, I might meet upwards of one hundred people. I certainly couldn't remember everyone's faces, but they usually remembered mine. And that was the scary thing. I wasn't sure if I'd dealt with him personally or if he'd been on the periphery of a job I'd done. Or maybe he was a complete stranger who hadn't come within spitting distance of me his entire life. Think of my paranoia as an occupational hazard.

I took a seat at the rear of the plane and asked Ross to sit next to me. He did. Mark sat two ahead of me, unaware of my concern. Alfonso sat directly in front of me, next to Ali.

I was still waiting on some divine intervention as to

Alfonso's identity, so my muddled mind decided on a costume change.

'Jesus it's hot in here, hey Ross,' I said. 'Fuck this for a joke.' I then took off my T-shirt and wrapped it over my head. I completed my new look with a cap over the top. It gave me that bare-chested French Foreign Legion look, and hopefully offered some disguise when Alfonso turned around, no matter how ineffectual it probably was in reality.

'Good idea,' Ross replied.

He then followed my lead, slipping out of his ill-fitting suit and throwing on a change of clothes more appropriate for the tropical clime. Everyone pleased with their attire, Jimmy fired up the Piper and we were away. Ten minutes later we were flying at 10 000 feet, settled in for four hours of AC/DC playing live in the skies. Actually, Bon and the boys I could handle; the decibels of AC/DC without the music itself, I couldn't.

Even though talking was shouting and hearing was redundant, Ross felt it was his duty to hold court in the two back seats of the plane. It pissed me off. If Ross was quiet, there would definitely be a lesser likelihood of Alfonso turning around and joining in the conversation. But no such luck.

'Now Jim's gonna go up to New Guinea a few days before we do it, you know, to sort out any loose ends. You know, brother Ben, if he goes a few days before, it doesn't look suspicious. Maybe take his family, who knows?'

'Yeah, good idea,' I yelled back, preparing myself for an intervention.

'Hey Jim,' shouted Ross, 'when are you going to New Guinea again?'

Alfonso turned around. On cue I spun my face towards Ross, giving Jim a side profile, my T-shirt partially obscuring my features. 'I thought maybe a few days beforehand,' he replied. 'What do you think?'

'Good, good,' Ross roared in return.

'It's not suspicious that way, yeah,' Jim replied, looking at me and then Ross in turn. I nodded, clocking his face for a second. It momentarily calmed me. I had a feeling I'd freaked myself out over this bloke. Sure he looked familiar, but in a stressful situation, the whole problem had probably been compounded. It also helped that Jim Alfonso was from Griffith and not Melbourne. His criminal network was different than that of, say, Twin's John Dugdale.

'That's the way, Jim,' bellowed Ross. 'Yeah, just a few days, yeah.'

After an hour of airtime, Mark stumbled and stooped down to the back of the plane for a chat to break up the boredom. He'd been poring over maps at the front of the plane, but there was no available seat for him down the back, so he crouched in the aisle next to Ross. For the first time in a long time, I was kind of happy to see him. When we were alone he was unbearable, but when we were with the targets, at least he couldn't make me paranoid. Mind you, with Jim Alfonso sitting in front of me, I'd already done a good job of that myself without Mark in my ear.

'So how are you related to Jim?' Mark yelled.

'Just a friend, a business friend,' Ross replied.

'Not family?'

'He's family, yes, but he's ... we're all family working together, you know.'

Mark looked confused. A moment later he asked a question that was capable of giving us some damning evidence about organised crime in this country. 'There's one thing I've always wanted to ask you, Ross. Are you the Mafia? Or is that just on the television, you know?'

Undercover

'All we are is family, Mark,' shouted Ross. 'We're a group of people who get together to do things like this, you know, do some business on Horn Island. We don't call it the Mafia.'

'How come?' I joined in. This was getting interesting.

'You know, brother Ben, "Mafia" is a very bad word. The minute you say "Mafia", you know, very bad. We are family. Family's very good. Family look after each other. Like that man in Adelaide. The police building.'

'What? What police building?' I asked.

'The police building that was blown up. They hit one of our guys hard,' Ross replied. 'We had to do it.'

Shit. Ross Trimboli was talking about the bombing of the National Crime Authority headquarters in Adelaide about two months before. A parcel had arrived at the building, and when an investigator opened it the explosion killed him instantly. Shards of glass from the twelfth floor windows rained down on pedestrians walking by. Several were hospitalised as a result of their injuries. It was just pure luck that others weren't killed in the carnage inside the building.

To be honest, that admission by Ross affected me badly. What a prick. For a bloke who crapped on about family all the time, I felt like he'd just confessed to killing one of my own family. I know it sounds a bit dicky, but I loved the brotherhood of the police force. People genuinely looked after each other through good and bad. At that time it couldn't have been spelled out to me any clearer: his family was at war with my family. And fuck him.

'So are the family just in Griffith?' Mark asked.

'No, we have family everywhere, Mark. All over Australia, the world.'

'What, in all the cities?'

'All the big ones, yes, and Griffith, of course.'
'What about back in Italy?' I asked.
'Of course we have contact with our family in Calabria,' said Ross.
'So how often do you get together?' Mark asked.
'We only come together when we have to. Usually when something bad has happened to the family.'
Expect a meeting soon then, Ross. Like when we bust you and your mates for importing a tonne of cannabis into the country. Just don't expect an invite.
Half an hour later, Ross was shooting his mouth off again. I was just hoping that the in-flight microphones were picking it all up. It was incriminating stuff.
'What are we doing about the customs officer at Horn Island?' Alfonso asked Ross through the crack in the seats in front of us. I looked away from him, but not so pronouncedly this time. If he hadn't identified me by now, I could start to feel a bit safer.
'We'll take the risk,' Ross replied by way of a shout. 'It's a Sunday morning, Jim, as you know, before dawn. He won't be there, but if he interferes, we'll just kill him. Take him up in the plane and throw him out.'
News to us. Last time we discussed the customs bloke at Horn Island, he was on the take. It looked like he wasn't any more. I guess Ross figured that he was one less expense to worry about.
'Have you presold the rest of the cannabis?' I asked.
'Most of it's sold, yeah.'
''Cause I was hoping to get more of it as well. I'm not sure how much. Maybe 5000 a kilo after that first fifty,' I said, knowing that we'd shored up fifty kilograms of the shipment already. Courtesy of telephone intercepts that had come through Special Projects Unit, I knew that Ross and

Tony had already been selling the cannabis sight unseen at $8000 a kilo.

'Um, that sounds about right, I think,' he replied. 'There won't be much though. Most of it's gone.'

The next hour or two on the plane was boring stuff, and when we approached Horn Island at dusk, I'd just about had it with the Piper. My eardrums were ready to burst. By that stage I wouldn't have cared if Jim Alfonso pulled a gun on me when we hit land if it meant I wouldn't have to get back in the noisy bloody thing.

I'd already mentioned to Ross and Mark that I was struggling with the racket, and Mark was kind enough to offer to switch possies with me once we got back to Cairns. I'd be flying Bob Dylan, and he'd continue listening to Acca Dacca all the way down to Melbourne. It was quite the noble gesture on his part.

In a textbook landing, Jimmy brought the plane down on Horn Island under the cover of darkness. He was the first out of the craft, busily making himself busy, busy, busy. First he checked the wheels, then the wings, then the engine. After all that, it was time to refuel. The man was a machine. Anything but talk to the gangsters, was his philosophy.

When we stepped foot off the plane, the airstrip was deathly quiet except for the sounds of bugs chirping away in the humidity of the warm night air. It didn't go unnoticed.

'Listen to that, everyone,' said Ross, standing in the middle of the tarmac. We all looked around for the source of a sound that didn't exist. 'It's quiet. Bloody quiet. Good, good, yeah. Guys, make your way over here.'

While we all walked in small circles stretching our legs, Ross thought it was a good time for a powwow. I was just happy that Jim hadn't reached for a gun. Maybe my overactive imagination had caught up with me again. But, looking over at Alfonso, there was still something about him that was known to me. He was dark and strong, yet standoffish. He had a bit of presence about him, something a lot of the Griffith Mafia lacked. He looked like a lot of the Italians I went to school with growing up. Maybe that's why I freaked out.

'The chopper will take about twenty minutes to half an hour to get here,' said Ross, his voice still raised because of the last four hours of shouting. 'It'll be here at five in the morning, five minutes after we land.'

'And it's an army chopper, yeah?' I asked.

'Yes, brother Ben. Ali sorted that out. He was in the army.'

Ali from the PNG Army nodded, an infectiously goofy grin on his face. We all nodded back, with goofy grins of our own. On reflection, Ali was a funny one. When I'd spoken to him on the plane for a minute earlier in the day, the conversation had gone a little like this:

'So you're gonna bring it down, Ali?' I asked, alluding to the chopper full of grass that would be flying into Horn Island from New Guinea.

He started giggling for no reason. 'Yeah, yeah.'

'How long do you think it will take?' I asked, starting to laugh at him laughing.

'Twenty minutes.' More giggles.

'Rightio mate.'

Fucken thigh-slapper. That was the end of our conversation, but I couldn't work it out. Was the bloke ripped off his face? Or am I funnier than I give myself credit for?

Anyway, back to Ross on the Horn Island tarmac. 'It should take no longer than four minutes to load up this plane.'

Undercover

'I think you'll find it takes ten minutes, Ross,' Mark corrected him.

'Whatever, four, five, ten, I'm just saying that we'll be quick.'

'Yeah, you'd better make sure of that,' Mark said, looking around to see where our pilot was. Jimmy had his head under one of the wheels a good 50 metres away. 'Jimmy will take off just like that, you know. He doesn't even want to know what the cargo is. Doesn't give a shit. Could be boomerangs for all he cares. He just wants to get the plane back up in the air as quickly as possible.'

'Yes, that's why I said four minutes. Now when the plane gets to Cohuna, it will take what?' asked a sarcastic Ross, looking over at Mark. 'Say, ten minutes to unload the lot, yeah? We'll have more than enough cars to carry the gear.'

'Do we need to know anything about the drive back to Griffith?' I asked.

'It'll work like this: we'll put grass in one car, and then nothing in the next one. You know, repeat that. Five cars with grass, five without. We'll space them apart every few minutes. That way if the police pull over one car, we have a fifty-fifty chance.'

'What if they pull over a car with the grass in it?' I asked.

'Well, then the next car that comes along can shoot them,' replied Ross. As easy as that.

'What if there's more than one cop car on the road?'

'What, together? Impossible. The coppers work that road alone. By the time the bodies are discovered, we'll be home.'

'So we kill them, no questions asked?'

'No, brother Ben. A few of us will be carrying thirty grand in cash, you know, to pay them off. If the coppers are too stupid to take the money, that's their choice.' Ross then looked around. In the background, Jimmy was firing up the vehicle for its return voyage. 'Any questions before we go?'

Nothing stirred except for the thunderclap of the Piper's twin engines.

'Okay everyone, this is just the beginning. We'll do another shipment after this next one in two to three months,' said Ross. 'We want this to be a regular thing.'

We filed back to the plane, two of us well aware that, for once, what Ross wanted, Ross would not be getting.

Sixteen

17-19 June, 1994

Friday June 17, 3:30 a.m.
Knock, knock, knock.

Ross Trimboli was rapping on the front door of the East Melbourne apartment. At that time of the morning it felt more like a wake-up call than a house call, but he and Fifi Romeo were expected.

At nine o'clock the previous night, Ross had called me from Griffith to tell me that he was on his way down to Melbourne. He had a package to drop off. Over the telephone he wouldn't tell me exactly what he was delivering, but I'd had a fair idea anyway.

I'd called Mark and he popped over. For the last few hours we'd been channel surfing from infomercial to infomercial. When the boys came knocking, Mark was so spellbound by a blonde demonstrating some useless piece of fitness equipment, he made me get up to answer the door.

'Evening, gents.'

Both of them looked tired, understandably so after six hours on the road in the middle of the night.

'Brother Ben,' Ross spoke in a half-whisper, 'I have those guns for you in the car. Is it okay to bring them in now?'

'Sure, not a problem.'

Ross darted back to his car while Fifi stood expectantly on the doorstep. 'Come in, Fifi. Mark is parked on the couch.'

After Fifi crashed next to Mark, Ross returned from the car. I ferried him through the doorway, the weapons wrapped in a towel under his arm.

The guns were for Mark to take with him to Horn Island in case someone required a close-up of a barrel when the grass was being picked up. The climax to Operation Afghan was less than forty-eight hours away, and Ross was just crossing a few Ts and dotting some Is before the big deal.

Ross had supplied two firearms and ammunition for me to put on the plane. One was a .38 pistol with 200 rounds. The other was a big boy, an M1 semiautomatic carbine with 300 rounds at his disposal. Ross figured a fuck-off machine gun should earn Mark some respect if the customs officer gave him any lip.

'Here, brother Ben. These are for Mark.' He handed over the guns.

'Yeah, I'll just tuck them away somewhere,' I said, walking into the bedroom and placing them neatly on the floor.

'How are we all?' asked Ross as he shuffled into the living room.

'Good, good,' Mark said, preparing to lift himself off the couch. 'Everything's ready to go.'

'Don't get up, Mark. We're just on our way to the hotel.'

'Which one?' I asked.

'The Old Melbourne. You know it?'

'Sure,' Mark said.

'Good. We'll see the two of you there tomorrow. In a few hours, yeah?'

'No worries. I'll see you blokes out,' I said.

We walked out onto the street, and the two of them headed for Ross's red Porsche.

'I swear, Ross, I'm gonna get myself one of them after this job. It's a bloody chick magnet.'

Ross smiled as he lowered himself into the driver's seat. I'd buttered him up enough. It was time to hit him up.

'Listen mate, I've actually got a favour to ask,' I said. 'I might need something from you, some coke. As much as you can get on short notice.'

'When for?' he asked.

'A.s.a.p. Tomorrow, I mean, today would be good,' I said, glancing at my watch.

'I'll see what I can do. Shouldn't be a problem.'

'Great, but if you could just keep it quiet at this stage,' I said, signalling back towards the house. 'I don't want Mark to know about it. Just got something on the side.'

'Are you sure?' Ross asked.

'Yeah, no drama, I just need some coke.'

'Okay, I'll make some calls for you. Ring me later when Mark leaves.' My paranoid brother was due to leave for Cairns in about seven hours' time.

'Sure. Just one other thing. Can I give you the money next week, if that's no problem, yeah?'

Ross smiled. 'Yeah, I think I can organise that.'

Sorted. I went back inside as Mark was making his way outside. 'I'm off then,' he said. 'Pick us up at eight, could you? We've got to be at Essendon Airport at eight-thirty. I just need some sleep.'

'See ya.'

I didn't particularly like keeping secrets from Mark, but he'd contributed to this situation. Just a day earlier he'd got wind of the fact that I'd been having conversations with Ross about buying more cocaine.

'Don't even think about doing any deals while I'm away,

okay,' he threatened. 'Because if something fucks up, the whole operation could be in jeopardy.'

I took what Mark said on board, but I also knew that the operation wasn't going to fuck up because of a cocaine deal on credit. This was a separate issue from the importation, and our controller Coach Cody agreed with me. I ignored Mark's advice.

The way I saw it, Ross would be under lock and key in a few days, and the more evidence we collected on him the better. I also knew that the bosses wouldn't approve any more money to buy drugs. The best way to get around that detail was to buy them on credit. The charges on Ross would be valid, and the public purse wouldn't be opened. What could be better? Personally, I thought the whole idea was a stroke of genius.

After a few hours of sleep, Mark and I rendezvoused with Coach Cody at Essendon Airport. Coach was overseeing a makeover of the Piper Navajo that would be flying to Horn Island in less than thirty hours. It was a different plane to the one that did the dry run, so the surveillance guys were called in again to fit it out with devices for the trip.

I walked onto the plane with a bag containing the machine gun, pistol and ammunition. After dumping the firearms we whizzed around to the Old Melbourne Hotel to pick up Griffith gangster Lindsay Boram, Mark's travelling partner to Cairns. Lindsay was a big bear of a man, a Riverina local, and a trusted footsoldier in the organisation. Along with Mark, his job was to keep an eye on the shipment of grass from Horn Island to Cohuna.

The two of them had to catch an 11 a.m. flight out of Tullamarine, connecting with Jimmy's Piper in Cairns the next evening. After the aural assault of the dummy run, Mark shrewdly opted to subject himself to the Piper only for the four-hour flight from Cairns to Horn Island.

On the way back from the airport I called Ross for an update. He was confident that he had a 'Picasso' for me to take a look at. In Griffith Mafia speak, the cocaine deal sounded like a goer. Seeing as I didn't have to pay for it, I was hoping that he'd managed to scrape together pounds and pounds of the stuff. We arranged to meet in the car park of the First and Last Hotel at one o'clock, in about an hour and a half's time.

I then dropped in on Coach again at Essendon Airport. When I'd been there a few hours earlier I was unable to discuss details of the coke deal because Mark was breathing down my neck.

'Okay, I've just spoken to Ross. He reckons he's tracked down some coke for me, you know, the deal on credit.'

'Good, buddy. When are you doing it?'

'In an hour or so. I told him to keep it quiet, you know, keep it from Mark.'

'Yeah, that's probably a good thing. Don't push it too hard though. If they've got it, fine, but if they haven't, just forget about it.'

'No worries.'

'And we'll have to tell Mark about it later. Just in case someone drops it into the conversation.'

'Yeah, but wait until the deal's been done, yeah,' I said.

I left Coach at the airport, and made my way to the Fawkner pub. At 1:10 p.m. I drove into the car park, wired and ready to deal. The red Porsche was already there, Ross Trimboli and the two Rocco Romeos, Fifi and Roy, squished inside. I made my way over to them.

'Jesus, Fifi, how did you get in there?'

Inside, poor Fifi's legs were splayed at right angles to his body. The 911 had a back seat, but it must've been some sort of cruel German automotive design joke. Sure, you could toss a tennis racquet in the back, but to fit in a whole Fifi Romeo was playing havoc with the car's design capabilities.

'Jump in my car, guys,' I said. 'I think I can fit you all in.'

The three of them tumbled out of the car, Fifi the most relieved of them all.

'Sorry I'm late,' I said to Ross. 'Bloody traffic.'

'No problem. We only just arrived ourselves,' he responded, jumping in the front seat of my blue Commodore.

'Otherwise I would've got out of that bloody car earlier,' said a puffed-out Fifi. Extricating himself limb by limb from the Porsche's backseat had taken the wind out of the poor fella.

'Well, how do you want to do this?' I asked.

'We'll just go for a drive, yeah,' answered Ross.

For a few minutes I tentatively negotiated the Fawkner back streets, Ross and Fifi barking last-minute navigational instructions. Then they made me park outside a row of shops. Fifi stepped out of the car and went for a stroll. I took it that he was grabbing the gear from his house. It was pretty much standard procedure to stay away from someone's residence when conducting a deal.

'He'll be back with it in a minute,' Ross confirmed.

'How much could you get your hands on?'

'Half a pound.'

'I really appreciate this, Ross. I'll fix you up next week, no worries. How much are we looking at?'

'Forty.' That's thousands of dollars. Not a bad price for close to a quarter of a kilo.

Undercover

'Forty. Not a problem,' I said.

'You're right, brother Ben. It's not a problem. I can trust you,' said Ross, coming over all sentimental on me. 'We'll be doing a lot of things together in the future. We're like brothers now.'

The whole scene was taking on a surreal feel, especially with silent Roy sitting remotely in the back seat, but I thought I'd better reciprocate without sounding too sucky. 'Thanks Ross. It's just such a relief to do business with people who don't fuck you around.'

'Of course. You and Mark are like family now. Why would we fuck around family?' asked Ross — rhetorically, I presumed.

'It's great. When you meet some people, you just know you can trust them, you know, you want to be around them.'

'Yes, brother Ben. That's what family's all about.'

Fifi then interrupted the lovefest, a small clear plastic bag of cocaine in his hand wrapped in a blue handkerchief, thankfully unused. He handed it over to me from the back seat.

'It's pure. Very good stuff,' he said.

'Thanks mate. Thanks a lot.'

I then drove Ross and Roy back to the Porsche. After the back-seat trauma of half an hour ago, Fifi wisely decided to make the return journey to his house on foot. Once I'd dropped them off, I took off for Coach back at Essendon Airport. I had to hand over the cocaine.

'Good work, buddy. Goes well with the kilo we got earlier,' he said.

'Got it for forty grand.'

'I think you'll find free is always a good price, buddy,' Coach quipped.

Damian Marrett

It was about two-thirty, so I returned to the office to catch up on some paperwork. The eleventh-hour cocaine deal had given me a real boost. It was significant because it would make them look stupid in court. I'd well and truly shoved it up their arses.

That night I slept uneasily, a bit toey about what the next forty-eight hours had in store. The next day I would be heading up to Griffith, holding the fort while Mark, Jimmy and Lindsay Boram flew the grass back down south to Cohuna. But the most exciting thing for me personally was that the whole operation was finally going to be over. I'd had more than enough of Afghan.

The next morning I arrived in the office at nine forty-five. I fixed myself a coffee, and whipped Coach's arse in a quick hit of office cricket. Coach's chicken legs couldn't hack the pace as I dispatched him to all four corners of the room.

At ten-thirty I cleared to Griffith by myself. It was a very pleasant drive listening to the footy on the radio without Mark reaching for the off switch. Around about 5 p.m. I arrived in Leeton, about 60 kilometres east of Griffith. We'd booked accommodation there for the night.

Coach arrived an hour later with some news from Mark. 'I've had a chat to him about the coke deal,' he said.

'How was he?'

'Well, I could tell he wasn't happy about it, buddy.'

'We already knew that, Coach.'

'He'll be fine. I think he's just pissed off 'cause we didn't tell him about it.'

'Like it would've happened if we'd told him about it.'

'I know, I know.'

Coach also told me that at Narrandera, about 80 km southeast of Griffith, around 100 police from Victoria and

New South Wales were already assembling. They had cover for their strength in numbers: the annual golf weekend for coppers and publicans had been scheduled weeks in advance.

That night, the Narrandera 100 conducted a mass briefing. The operation commander from NSW, a Chief Inspector, held the floor. 'Now, before we get down to business, let's make a deal. If you boys don't kill anyone, we won't steal anything.' The in-joke brought the house down. At that time the Victoria Police had a reputation, rightly or wrongly, for shooting first, asking questions later. Our northern counterparts were perpetually under the spotlight for corruption and graft.

While the briefing was going on, I drove over to Ross Trimboli's house ten minutes south of Griffith. We took a seat in the living room, Ross's wife plying us with salami and Saladas.

'So, any word from New Guinea yet?' I asked.

'No, but it's all ready. It's all worked out. We've had to drop the weight from a tonne to 750 kilos though. Worried about the chopper handling it.'

'Shit, will that affect our amounts?'

'No, you and Mark come first, brother Ben. We'll look after you before anyone else.'

'Thanks Ross.'

'I'll get a phone call as soon as the chopper lands tomorrow. Then we'll go from there, but I'll ring you when it's on its way.'

After a few rounds of scotch, Ross started getting all soppy again. I guess it was a natural progression from the conversation we had in the car the day before. Again, family and loyalty were high on his agenda.

'Trust is the most important thing in business. I know I can trust you because, you know, you are family now. I love you like a brother, brother Ben,' he blabbed, the last three words coming out like 'bada bada bing'.

Steady on there, tiger, I thought to myself. But to be truthful, I did feel sorry for the guy a little bit. There was a real fondness in his voice. He was genuine, and I was very mindful of the fact that I wasn't. Italians are very generous, and it can be exhausting work busting someone when they're serving you food and drink all the time. I also knew that his immediate family would be tipped upside down when we chucked him in jail. I knew I shouldn't care, but throughout the operation I'd found it increasingly difficult to maintain my focus. Although it did become a lot easier after he'd recounted the Mafia's role in the NCA bombing.

At about midnight I left Ross Trimboli for the final time. Under the auspices of Operation Afghan, I never saw him as a free man again.

While I was safely tucked away snoring in a Leeton motel room with just my gun for company, Mark, Jimmy and Lindsay Boram were preparing to fly into Horn Island. The chopper full of grass was due to arrive at 5 a.m.

Jimmy landed the Piper on schedule at 4:55 a.m. While he busied himself refuelling, Mark and Boram awaited the helicopter's arrival outside the plane. After more than four hours in the air, Boram was desperate to take a piss.

He walked off to the side of the airstrip, and down a slight embankment for a bit of extra privacy. Unbeknownst to him, in his path lay one of our SOG boys. Well camouflaged, he'd dug himself in under some leaves. Before he had a chance to unzip his fly, Boram clumsily stumbled over this bloke's torso. On reflection, our man was probably too well camouflaged, but what can you do?

The jig was up.

Immediately Boram was taken into custody. We had no choice. He was taken peacefully, but he wasn't too keen on cooperating. In fact, once Mark revealed himself as an undercover, Boram gave him the silent treatment.

In all the commotion, the time ticked along to five-thirty, and the chopper still hadn't arrived. Mark was worried that Boram may have been given specific instructions that he had to make a phone call to a contact in New Guinea before the grass would be shifted.

Time was getting ahead of them. For a good hour, Mark tried to convince Boram to speak. No go. He asked him if a phone call was required before the chopper would turn up. Silence. Mark then suggested rather forcefully that making a phone call could advance his cause at the trial. Still the same resistance.

Back in Leeton, I woke up refreshed at seven, none the wiser. At eight-thirty, I gave Ross Trimboli a call. Coach was sitting beside me.

'G'day Ross. Have you heard anything yet?'

'Nothing. I don't know what's going on. I can't get hold of my man.'

'I'm worried about Mark. He hasn't rung me.'

'Don't worry, brother Ben. Mark will be all right. I'll make some more calls and get hold of my man.'

Ten minutes later, Coach took a call. It was Mark with the bad news. Boram was in custody, and they'd waited and waited, but the chopper hadn't arrived. It looked like there'd be no return flight. There was only one consolation: I wouldn't be breaking my back unloading cannabis at Cohuna later that day.

Once that call came through, we had to move fast. Although the plane full of grass wouldn't be making an appearance, the conspiracy to import a plane full of grass was a very serious charge. I had to ring Ross Trimboli again.

'Sorry Ross, but I'm starting to get a bit worried now, you know. Have you heard anything?'

'No, I don't know what's happened.'

'Shit, what are we gonna do?'

'All I know is that the chopper hasn't turned up yet. I don't think any phones are working up there. We'll just have to wait, brother Ben. Don't worry. Mark will be okay.'

'Should I just stay where I am?'

'Yeah, stay there. I'll tell you when anything happens. I'm going to meet with the other boys now.'

That's what we were waiting to hear. We knew that a meeting with all in attendance would be the perfect time to pounce.

Fifteen minutes later, six local men were taking a quiet Sunday morning stroll on Griffith's main thoroughfare, Banna Street. They were about to step into Benson's for some coffee and conversation. Two unmarked vans slowly pulled up beside them. In a flash, dozens of SOG ninjas poured out the back, guns poised. 'Get down on the ground, don't move, don't move.' No one moved. Everyone was scooped up without resistance.

Among the arrests were the Trimbolis (Ross and Domenic), Tony Romeo and Jim Alfonso. The only one missing was Rocco 'Roy' Romeo. In a strange way, it was typical of Roy to miss out on all the action. I have no idea what he was up to, but four days later he voluntarily gave himself up to Griffith police. I don't know why, but I like to think he lived off the land while he was on the run.

Raids were carried out at everyone's addresses. Ross's house unearthed 420 grams of cannabis, 55 grams of cocaine and rounds of ammunition. As always, Tony was far too clever to leave himself open; just a small plastic bag containing cannabis was seized at his home address.

Lindsay Boram wasn't spared. While he was under arrest on Horn Island, his house was turned upside down. Six plastic bags containing cannabis, a quantity of cannabis seeds, two cannabis plants, $950 in cash, and three long-arms and ammunition were discovered.

The farmhouse of my nemesis in the Piper, Jim 'Familiar' Alfonso, netted 23 grams of cannabis, four long-arms, ammunition and $3600 in cash. Ross's brother Domenic's house came back relatively clean — only documents seized, along with $565.35 in cash.

Documents were also snared from both Tony's and Ross's houses. The Griffith Mafia's accountant was targeted as well. His Griffith office contained a mountain of documents tracing the organisation's money-laundering activities.

Simultaneous raids were progressing in Melbourne. Rocco 'Fifi' Romeo and Pat Agresta were both nabbed at their home addresses. Fifi was caught with six pounds of cannabis, four long-arms and ammunition, just under $1800 in cash, scales, and plastic bags for drug dealing. Located at Pat's premises were cannabis, seeds, foils of cocaine and $6600 in cash.

A total of 257 law enforcement officers raided seventeen homes and businesses in Victoria and New South Wales. Ten offenders were arrested, and nine were eventually charged with thirty-six offences in three different states — Victoria, NSW and Queensland.

While all this was happening, I was tucked away safely in my Leeton motel room. My job was already done, but I enjoyed hearing all the feedback from the busts. Sure, it was disappointing that the operation hadn't played out to its intended conclusion, but we were overjoyed all the same. The Griffith crime syndicate had already sold us over $250 000 worth of drugs in the months preceding, and we had more than enough evidence to put these blokes away on a conspiracy to import charge. From all quarters, the operation was deemed a success.

That night, Victoria Police's Assistant Commissioner Neil O'Loughlin was quoted as saying that the operation had uncovered 'a lot of evidence in relation to the trafficking of marijuana and cocaine within Australia'. Furthermore he went on to say, 'Nationwide, I think we have done an excellent job, and I think it's of no consequence that we didn't actually seize the 750 kilograms'.

In the next few days we pondered why the operation broke down at the final hurdle. Of course, Lindsay Boram's early-morning stumble was the logical explanation but, behind the scenes, there were other potential reasons for the chopper no-show.

Seven law enforcement and government agencies were involved in Operation Afghan — the Victoria Police Drug Squad, the NSW Police Organised Crime Unit, the Queensland Police Service, the National Crime Authority, the Australian Federal Police, the Australian Taxation Office and Australian Customs. This was the problem. We lost control of the operation once it left Victoria. With so many agencies involved, it just became too cumbersome.

A good example of this was the morning of the New Guinea airlift. The Queensland Police had involved the Royal Australian Navy for no good reason, and the radio airwaves that morning were full of white noise. There was more activity over the air than the police assistance call centre on a Saturday night. It would've alerted anybody attempting to smuggle contraband. Quite possibly our New Guinean couriers picked up on it, and stayed home.

Two weeks later a backslapping, boozy lunch was convened at Amarretto Restaurant in East Melbourne. The bigwigs at the NCA and Rover Taskforce took it upon themselves to shout the team a meal as a thank you for a job well done.

At the table one of the NCA bosses told us that, in their organisation's opinion, the Griffith Mafia was in some way responsible for at least five underworld deaths in the past fifteen years. It was a comforting thought that we'd finally managed to ping them for something.

After the meal, Inspector Rod Collins from the Rover Taskforce pulled me aside for a chat. 'Kid, we know that it was a stressful job, but we're going to look after you. We've got some money in the budget, so if you want to book yourself a holiday for a few grand, we'll pick up the tab.'

Nice one.

All in all, the lunch was a welcome respite from the tedium of transcription. I'd been at it for two weeks solid while Mark swanned about, working on components of the brief. Once again, he'd nabbed the good job. Rank has its privileges, I suppose.

Mark and I were fine after the job wound up. Although there was still some underlying tension between us, it had eased somewhat since the arrests. Now that we weren't in each other's faces twenty-four hours a day, it was a mighty relief.

I was just thankful that there was no more staying in character for weeks at a time. It was possible to now lay Ben Gleeson to rest. For the first time in more than six months, I was Damian Marrett again. Until the next job.

Epilogue

Straight after the job, I thought I was okay with everything. I spent a weekend with two friends, and just recently I saw one of them again. She said I was far from okay at that time. Apparently I was hiding my gun in different places around the house for no reason.

A few weeks later the Rover Taskforce came through on that holiday, and I booked myself in on Hamilton Island. It was supposed to be ten days of rest and recreation, but I found it very difficult to rest and recreate. A car backfired on the island one night, and I remember hitting the deck.

Six weeks after the arrests, the nine accused were handed our brief. That's when the penny well and truly dropped. They now had clear evidence before them that they'd been duped by a pair of undercovers. Most of them were proud people; it must have been humiliating.

Just days before the committal hearing at the Melbourne Magistrates Court, the phone rang at my home in Elwood. A voice I couldn't place was on the other end.

'Damian?'

'Yes.'

'Ben Gleeson?'

'Who's this?' I was still unsure if it was a workmate taking the piss.

'Mate, I was wondering if you might be interested in something.'

'Well, who am I talking to first?'
'I'm speaking for some friends.'
'What friends?'
'They've got big money for the tapes.'
'What fucken tapes?'
'The Griffith tapes, all of them,' the voice said. He was talking about the wires, taps and intercepts we'd recorded over the duration of the operation. Pretty much all the evidence we had collected on the Griffith Mafia.
'You're kidding?'
'Does 360 grand sound like I'm kidding?' No, but it was a bloody strange amount. I gathered the voice was that of an intermediary who was skimming off the top. The original amount was more likely to be 400 or 500 grand.
'Not interested. Next time show your face, okay, pal.'
'You want to think about it? Is it about more money?' the voice asked.
I hung up the phone.
At the committal hearing I was in the box for five days. My character was brought into question time and time again. Their barristers called me a professional liar, someone who couldn't be relied upon to tell the truth. I told them that I lied for a purpose: it was my job to play the part of a drug dealer. I had a reason to lie to our targets, but I had no reason to lie in court. It was the truth, and there were tapes to back it up.
There was a truckload of evidence to support our claims, so the lawyers took another tack. They tried to make out that we were international playboys flying around, snorting coke, screwing hookers, generally enjoying ourselves at taxpayers' expense. Their character assassinations didn't wash with the magistrate either.

Damian Marrett

Every day, the Mafia wives sat in court trying to support their husbands; these same women who had been cooking me breakfasts for months. When it came out in court that their husbands were rooting around on them, there were plenty of tears. Big cracks were appearing all the time, especially in Ross's marriage. Recordings were played for the court to hear, and just about every one of his telephone conversations would end the same way: 'Look, I've gotta go. I've got a girl coming round.'

Tony Romeo's demeanour in court surprised me. I truly expected him to retain some class and dignity, but he had all the grace of a meathead picking fights at the football. He snarled the whole time. I knew he'd lost everything, but I was a little bit disappointed. In a strange way I respected him, and I'd hoped that he'd be able to carry it off through thick and thin.

Maybe I stupidly thought he had some respect for me. But he didn't. He just wanted to kill me. While I was in the box he made an action towards me that suggested he wanted to slit my throat. It didn't bother me, but I let the prosecutors know anyway. The magistrate was then made aware that he'd done it, and he called in Romeo's counsel to admonish them. There was no way I was going to let him threaten me in that way.

The lot of them had excellent legal teams. They kept applying for bail. I recall one of the barristers saying, 'This is wrong. We're treating these men like dangerous criminals.'

'That's because they are,' I replied.

The evidence against them was compelling, and they all pleaded guilty. They simply couldn't see any way out. It was a huge relief. I could now concentrate fully on other operations that were in progress, the Afghan chapter of my life done and dusted.

Undercover

But the rifts still run deep in the Griffith Mafia.

Eight years after Afghan, in May 2002, Tony Romeo was released from jail. Six weeks later, on July 1, he was shot dead while pruning a tree in his Griffith orchard. Thirty people were in the vicinity of the hit. No one saw a thing.

GOING DOWN

List of Principal Charges and Sentences

Tony ROMEO
- Conspiracy to traffic a drug of dependence (cocaine and cannabis)
- Conspiracy to import a prohibited import (cannabis)

Sentence: 10 years

Ross TRIMBOLI
- Trafficking a drug of dependence (cocaine and cannabis)
- Conspiracy to traffic a drug of dependence (cocaine and cannabis)
- Conspiracy to import a prohibited import (cannabis)

Sentence: 10 years

Rocco 'Roy' ROMEO
- Trafficking a drug of dependence (cocaine)
- Conspiracy to traffic a drug of dependence (cocaine and cannabis)
- Conspiracy to import a prohibited import (cannabis)

Sentence: 4 years

Damian Marrett

Domenic TRIMBOLI
- Conspiracy to traffic a drug of dependence (cannabis)
- Conspiracy to import a prohibited import (cannabis)

Sentence: 3 years

Ignazio 'Jim' ALFONSO
- Conspiracy to traffic a drug of dependence (cannabis)
- Conspiracy to import a prohibited import (cannabis)

Sentence: 4 years

Lindsay BORAM
- Conspiracy to import a prohibited import (cannabis)
- Unlawful possession of a concealable firearm
- Unlicensed firearm

Sentence: 4 years

Rocco 'Fifi' ROMEO
- Trafficking a drug of dependence (cocaine x 2)
- Possessing a drug of dependence (cocaine x 2)
- Trafficking a drug of dependence (cannabis)
- Possessing a drug of dependence (cannabis)

Sentence: 3 years

Pasquale 'Pat' AGRESTA
- Conspiracy to traffic a drug of dependence (cocaine x 2)
- Conspiracy to traffic a drug of dependence (cannabis)
- Trafficking a drug of dependence

Sentence: 3 years

Never to be Released – Volume 3
Paul B. Kidd

Each year in Australia crimes are committed that are so evil their perpetrators are sentenced to the maximum punishment that the law allows. And seeing as there is no death penalty in any state of Australia, these worst-of-the-worst are sent to prison for life without the possibility of parole. It is termed 'never to be released'. To date, no criminal who has ever been handed down this sentence has been set free, and they will die in jail as the law demands.

But the fear of going to prison forever obviously does little to deter people from committing crimes of the most heinous nature. In his third book of case studies on the subject, Paul B. Kidd, a recognised authority on Australia's serial killers and criminals, looks at such cases as: the housewife who skinned her de-facto husband, cooked his head in a pot and served him up to his kids for dinner; a mild-mannered serial rapist and murderer who was so ordinary-looking that his victims trusted him immediately — time and time again; and a serial killer whose 'victim' turned up alive and well in the middle of his trial for her murder.

0 7322 6963 6

Mafia Wife

Lynda Milito with Reg Potterton

The spellbinding Mafia memoir from Lynda Milito, wife of Gambino family captain Louie Milito.

Mafia Wife is an unforgettable, intimate portrayal of Lynda Milito's strong, but often harrowing, marriage to Mafia hit man Louie Milito. It is also a personal story about her own attraction to danger, her yearning to escape her mother's stifling care, family dysfunction, spousal abuse, helping Louie with his minor criminal exploits, and mental illness. She delves into her past and confronts the demons that led her to live the life she did, culminating in her husband's disappearance and death, her own struggle with manic depression, and estrangement from her two children.

Her story is full of startling revelations, intriguing characters, senseless killings, ominous answers and vignettes of life and death in America's Mafia — an inner sanctum and underworld of greed and power, with a veil of bloodshed and death always hovering above.

0 7322 7822 8

Mr Nasty

Cameron White

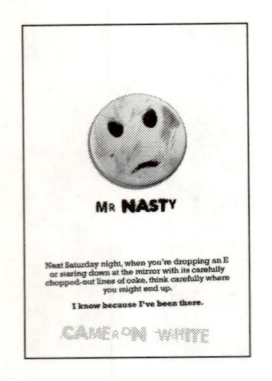

The rise, fall and ultimate redemption of a wannabe player in the global narcotics business.

Cameron White wasn't your archetypal drug dealer. He juggled a successful career as a talent and literary agent with an equally successful career as a dealer. Both paid well, but unfortunately he derived as much pleasure from partaking of the drugs as he did from the money he made from them.

A rational person, despite his addiction, he realised what he was getting into and repeatedly tried to run away, but wherever he went the drugs went with him — from New York to Los Angeles, Thailand, Berlin and Sydney.

It was only in Australia that he decided to turn his back for good on a life revolving around drugs. He could see that the global drug war had been lost and that radical action in the form of legislation was necessary in order to take the criminality out of the problem and turn it into a medical one. He returned to the UK and, avoiding his old stomping ground in London, checked himself into a clinic where he got the support he needed.

He has now been clean for three years and is waiting for the woman who supported him through his ordeal to join him from Sydney. His story is not glamorous, but rather gives an insight into what it is really like in the twilight world of dealers, users and abusers. He believes that there is light at the end of the tunnel for those caught in the downward spiral of drug use and this book shows that it is possible to reach it.

0 7322 8056 7